CREATIVE WRIT

MOST people at some time in their life are faced with the task of writing something entirely on their own, writing "creatively". It may be a letter, an essay, a review, or even, for the more ambitious, a story. Few find it an easy task, and so often a would-be author feels desperately that he has not been as successful as he could be, but is unsure where he has gone wrong, or how to improve his work.

John Freeman, the author of many articles and short stories, believes that many of these failures could be avoided and much potential literary skill now wasted could be saved and improved if only the fundamental skills of writing could be taught. His book is a highly successful attempt at achieving this. He presents a clear analysis of the structure and methods involved in the kind of writing which really appeals to readers, with special attention to the short story. Covering topics such as conflict, description, sentences and paragraphs, words, and style, he gives a firm indication of what is good and what should be avoided and illustrates his points by apt examples from successful pieces of literature.

It is clear from the outset that the profitable application of these skills depends entirely upon the personal efforts of the reader: throughout the book there are assignments linked with each topic, and an entire section illustrating the development in technique of a pupil of the author, with no previous experience, who worked through this method and is now a trainee editor for a group of magazines.

Although obviously written for aspiring young authors, every teacher will find in this unique work an encouragement for the dullest pupil, and every reader will find a valuable aid to improving their written style and sharpening their literary appreciation.

CREATIVE WRITING

JOHN F. FREEMAN, B.A.

FORMERLY ENGLISH MASTER AT
MARPLE HALL GRAMMAR SCHOOL

*With illustrative material by Kate Syme,
pupil of the above.*

FREDERICK MULLER LIMITED
LONDON

First published in Great Britain 1966
by Frederick Muller Limited, London, NW2 6LE

Reprinted 1977

ISBN 0 584 62006 3

British Library Cataloguing in Publication Data

Freeman, John Frederick
    Creative writing.
    1. Creative writing
    I. Title
    808'.042   PN193

    ISBN 0-584-62006-3

Printed in Great Britain by
Lowe & Brydone Printers Limited, Thetford, Norfolk

Contents

Acknowledgements

THE authors and publishers wish to thank the following for permission to quote from copyright material, the sources of which are individually acknowledged in the text: To Nigel Balchin and William Collins Sons & Co. Ltd., for the extract from *The Small Back Room*; to Caryl Brahms and S. J. Simon and Michael Joseph Ltd., for the extract from *A Bullet in the Ballet*; to J. Meade Faulkner and Edward Arnold Ltd., for the extract from *Moonfleet*; to Paul Gallico and Michael Joseph Ltd., for the extract from *The Snow Goose*; to Graham Greene and William Heinemann Ltd., for the extract from *The End of the Affair*; to the Executors of the late Sir Henry Rider Haggard and Cassell & Co. Ltd., for the extract from *King Solomon's Mines*; to Miss Jane Hope and Frederick Muller Ltd., for the extract from *Don't Do It!*; to Fred Hoyle and William Heinemann Ltd., for the extract from *The Black Cloud*; to Nigel Kneale and Penguin Books Ltd., for the extract from *Quatermass and the Pit*; to Miss Daphne du Maurier and Victor Gollancz Ltd., for the extract from *Rebecca*; to the Trustees of the Nevil Shute Norway Estate and William Heinemann & Co. Ltd., for the extract from *No Highway*; to Miss Dodie Smith and William Heinemann Ltd., for the extract from *I Capture the Castle*; to the Literary Executors of the Dylan Thomas Estate and J. M. Dent Ltd., for the extract from *Under Milk Wood*; to Russell Thorndyke and the Hutchinson Publishing Group, for the extract from *Dr. Syn*; to the Executors of the late H. G. Wells and Ernest Benn Ltd., for the extract from *In the Abyss* from the collection *The Short Stories of H. G. Wells*; to the executors of the late H. G. Wells and William Heinemann Ltd., for the extract from *The War of the Worlds*; to Mr. Otto Frank and Vallentine, Mitchell & Co., for the extract from *The Diary of Anne Frank*; and to the Estate of the late John Buchan and William Blackwood Ltd., for the extract from *The Thirty-Nine Steps*.

The authors would also like to acknowledge the help and encouragement of the members of the Stockport Writers' Circle.

Preface

WRITING is a mixture of two things. Firstly it is a skill. Secondly it is an art.

By a skill, I mean that there are correct ways of working which can be learnt.

By an art, I mean that some people have a special gift for writing, and that cannot be learnt.

Writing music is similar in many ways: before you start to write music you must learn about bars, notes, instruments and time signatures. This is the skill of composing music. Beethoven had to learn this.

But what distinguishes Beethoven from poorer composers is that he had musical imagination, musical ideas. No one could teach him those.

This book, then, sets out to teach you the skill of writing. Until you have learnt the skill, you will never know whether you are a real artist in words or not, just as Beethoven could not have known he would be an artist in music before he learnt the skills.

The skilled writer can always make the most of his ideas: the untrained, unskilled – however good he might have been as a word-artist – can never get anywhere.

Learning the skill of writing is hard work, but

when someone reads a piece of your writing and says: "That was good . . . or amusing . . . or exciting . . ." then I am sure you will think it well worth while.

Throughout this book special attention has been paid to writing short stories, but all the points mentioned are applicable to every form of creative writing. A novel, an essay, even a report needs ideas, credibility, good description and use of words, and proper sentences and paragraphs. The important thing is to build up a lively and interesting style that will really interest your readers.

1 Conflict

BEFORE doing anything about *writing* a story, we shall have to consider exactly what a story *is*.

A story must be much more than a string of happenings written down. Think of what you have done already today – from the time you got up this morning. Certainly a lot of things will have happened to you – but if you were to write them all down the chances are that it would hardly be a story that you, or anyone else, would want to read. It would almost certainly lack excitement. Probably you can think of one day when your doings would make a good story – but it would be only one day among many.

So a story is going to be a selection of what happens in life – not what happens all the time.

Even if we deliberately put a bit of excitement into a story it can still sound very dull. Take this as an example:

> A man is riding through a mountain range on horseback. He finds a cave in the mountainside, and goes in. Inside he finds a chest full of treasure. He loads up his horse with the treasure, and rides back to town.

Certainly not an everyday occurrence – but how-

11

ever well you were to expand that theme into a complete story, it never looks as if it is really going to be thoroughly interesting.

By looking at the framework of a story in this way, we can see at a glance that it is hardly worth putting much time or effort into what is certain to be a dreary piece of writing. To start writing without checking your plan is to risk wasting time on a story that has an unsound plot.

Therefore we have to plan it at least in this sort of outline before starting.

Probably you have already had some ideas about what is wrong with the plan given above. Some possible adjustments might be:

> The cave falls in and traps him ... or ... someone tries to shoot him on his way back to town ... or ... the gold weighs down his horse so much that it collapses and he is left stranded in the desert.

Any of these would improve it. Therefore all these ideas must have something in common – some factor that adds interest to a story. We call this factor *conflict*. That simply means that someone is in some difficulty; that there is something in the story that he has to fight against. In the first instance it would be the rock that he would have to fight to get out. In the second, it would be a straight fight with the man with the gun. In the third, it would be the desert with which he was in conflict.

All stories, whether they are written in books, or for plays or films, must have a conflict.

So, when we start making a plan the first thing is to be sure that there is going to be a conflict in it. Some subjects have conflict almost automatically.

A war story obviously has conflict between the opposing sides. Any Western will have at least one gun-fight (in fact I cannot remember a Western with only one).

But the word "conflict", as applied to writing, does not necessarily mean fighting, in the violent sense. Frequently, the most interesting conflicts are between two people with opposing ideas: you would find this in a story about a court case, where the prosecution and defence are in conflict. Conflict can arise between a person and a thing: hospital stories where the doctors are in conflict with disease are an easy example.

Conflict can even arise within the mind of a single person, where he cannot decide what action to take. You could describe this as a fight with his own conscience.

Nevertheless, ready-made subjects like wars, cowboys and hospitals have been used so often that the ideas – good in themselves – are now rather tired and dull. It is far better to find some unlikely or unusual subject in which the conflict can develop. Moreover, your knowledge of wars, cowboys and surgery is far too limited.

We can also apply this principle of conflict to any story we read. Take *The War of the Worlds* by H. G. Wells. It starts very quietly. Some red flashes are seen by astronomers on the planet Mars. A little later large cylinders fall on the earth, and we learn that these flashes must have been the launching of the space-ships. One lands near London and a crowd gathers. The top of the cylinder begins to unscrew and a little later the Martian creatures are heard, busily at work in the pit where their cylinder landed. So far, no conflict. It has all been handled very quietly so that we are quite prepared to believe that it really happened. Then a deputation sets out to try to talk to the Martians to show them that they are welcome:

There has been some hasty consultation and, since the Martians were evidently, in spite of their repulsive forms, intelligent creatures, it had been resolved to show them with signals, that we, too, were intelligent.

Flutter, flutter, went the flag, first to the right then to the left. It was too far for me to discover anyone there, but afterwards I learnt that Ogilivy, Stent and Henderson were with the others in this attempt at communication. This little group had in its advance dragged inward, so to speak, the circumference of the now almost complete circle of people, and a number of dim black figures followed at discreet distances.

Suddenly there was a flash of light, and a quantity of luminous greenish smoke came out of the pit in three distinct puffs, which drove up, one after the other, straight into the still air.

This smoke (or flame perhaps would be a better word for it) was so bright that the deep blue sky overhead and the hazy stretches of brown common towards Chertsey, set with black pine trees, seemed to darken abruptly as these puffs arose, and to remain darker after their dispersal.

At the same time a faint hissing became audible. . . .

Then slowly the hissing passed into a long, loud droning noise. Slowly a humped figure rose out of the pit, and the ghost of a beam of light seemed to flicker from it.

Forthwith flashes of actual flame, a bright glare leaping from one to another, sprang from the scattered group of men. It was as if some invisible jet impinged upon them and flashed into white flame. It was as if each man suddenly and momentarily turned to fire.

Then by the light of their own destruction, I saw them staggering and falling, and their supporters turning to run.

I stood staring, not as yet realising that this was death leaping from man to man in that distant crowd. . . .

14

The conflict has started: between the Martians and the people on Earth. We can see why the title was *The War of the Worlds*. It is this battle which is fought out through the whole of the book: one of the first examples, and one of the finest, of Science Fiction.

To set out the theme diagrammatically would give this result:

Earthmen ———————— Martians
Conquest of the Earth

i.e. There are two sides in conflict and the subject of the conflict is conquest of the earth.

Even in the simplest, most childish stories the same principle will hold:

Snow White ————— Wicked Queen
Jealousy (of Snow White's beauty)

So far, our plan must consist of two sides, which are in conflict, and a reason for that conflict.

There is one more factor that we must bring in, right at the planning stage. We have to know, before we can really settle down to write the story, who is going to win, and why. After all, anyone who reads your story is going to be waiting for the ending: they want to know what happens at the end – just as, if you have not read the book, you may want to know whether or not the Martians win in *The War of the Worlds*.

This other point will complete a *triangle of conflict*. Once more, a brief story outline: Cassius and Brutus have just killed Julius Caesar, because they were afraid that he would become king of Rome. Mark Antony, Caesar's greatest friend, is given permission to speak at Caesar's funeral and, appealing to the

15

people's greed by telling them Caesar has left them all his possessions in his will, persuades them to drive Cassius and Brutus out of Rome.

In diagram form, the story can be set out like this:

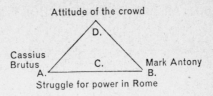

A full plan requires (a) and (b) two sides in conflict, (c) a reason for the conflict, and (d) a deciding factor, which controls the outcome of the conflict.

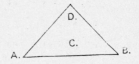

We might now have a look at another author solving the problem of the outcome of the conflict, and showing his readers the deciding factor that they have been waiting for since the conflict started. This is from *Dr. Syn* by Russell Thorndyke.

Dr. Syn, the local preacher, a former pirate and still a smuggler, has been betrayed to the Redcoats as Clegg the pirate, by Morgan Walters. The Redcoats have invaded the church during the service, and Dr. Syn, alias Clegg, preaching from the pulpit, has drawn his pistols on the Captain warning him to let him go. Then he tries to make his escape. He has not forgotten Morgan Walters either – the man who betrayed him.

Dr. Syn deliberately thrust both his pistols beneath his black gown. At the same moment the Captain sprang at the pulpit, but was knocked over with a violent blow from the brass candlestick that Dr. Syn had snatched from its socket. The sailors clambered out of their pews, but were met with a volley of hymn-books and hassocks from the salts in the choir. One or two pistols flashed, and in a second the entire church was a writhing, fighting mass of men. The women screamed and were trodden down as Redcoats entered the west door and forced their way over the upturned benches in the aisles. Above the congregation flew a medley of missiles – hassocks, books, hats, sticks, anything that could be grabbed, went flying through the air; and Syn leaped from the pulpit and fell upon the writhing mass that was fighting below.

It took the Redcoats a quarter of an hour to restore order in the church; and then Mr. Mipps and Dr. Syn had disappeared.

But although Collyer was very badly cut and bruised, he was confident; for the church had been surrounded, so he knew that the miscreants couldn't escape. Presently a cry from the vestry rang out –

"Help!"

It was Mipps's voice. Collyer rushed to the door, followed by some of his men. The remaining Redcoats, who had been watching the church, were ordered inside to help in the arrest. These men cried out that they had seen the Doctor in the vestry from the window, and were one and all eager to be in at the death.

Within the vestry stood Sexton Mipps with a blunderbuss at the head of Dr. Syn, who was crouched in terror at the old oak table.

"There he is. Seize him! – the devil! The murderer! Seize him."

"So you've turned King's evidence after all, have you, Mr. Sexton?"

But Mipps only cried again:

"There he is. Ain't none of you a-goin' to take him?"

Captain Collyer obeyed the Sexton and cried:

17

"Clegg, I arrest you in the name of the King!" and, coming forward, he laid his hand on the Doctor's shoulder. But the Doctor did not move. The Captain shook him but he did not move. The Captain put his hand on the white hair, and the Captain's hand was covered with something white.

"My God," he cried, "he's nailed to the table. It's not Syn – it's Morgan Walters. Where's that damned Sexton?"

But the Sexton had disappeared, and Clegg had gone, and there, with three nails – one through the neck, and one through each arm, driven right into the table, lay the theatrical figure of Morgan Walters, in all points resembling Doctor Syn.

Here there are two conflicts: the main one between Syn and the Redcoats and another between Syn and Morgan Walters, the informer. Both are solved by the same deciding factor: the trick of dressing Walters up as Syn, and so getting the surrounding soldiers to relax their guard.

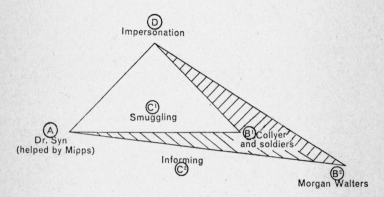

The last point to be considered is this. Although you are the author of your own story, and so can control what the characters do, there is one thing that is

18

rarely very successful. That is to make the deciding factor *luck*. Just because you have got your characters into such a tangle that it seems there is no possible solution, it is unfair to wave a little magic wand and introduce, quite out of the blue, some piece of luck that solves everything.

For example:

> Girl is in conflict with one of her school-friends over who shall get the main part in a school play. She knows she is not good at acting but is desperately keen to get the part. At first she is not chosen, but then her friend breaks a leg, and so she is given the part.

How lucky! Perhaps such things do happen, but it is hardly convincing as a story. The author's only solution was to remove the conflict altogether. If we rephrase the story like this:

> Girl in conflict with school friend over who shall get the main part in a school play. She knows she is not as good at acting, but is desperately keen to get the part. She practises at home, and on her way to school. Even when the audition comes she is far from satisfied with her own performance, and it is still not as good as that of her friend. Nevertheless, she is given the part, on the grounds that since she has improved so much already, by the time the rehearsals are over, she will be far better than her friend.

Now the conflict is kept up, and strengthened. The ending, too, is more convincing – less of a let-down.

There are four factors required: two factors in conflict, a reason for the conflict, and a deciding factor, which must not be luck.

Assignment 1
(1) Try and work out the conflict triangle for any

book you have read recently. Do the same with a television programme: perhaps one of the police, or hospital type.

(2) Work out a conflict triangle for a story of your own, either by making up the triangle, and building a story outline round it; or by thinking of a story and then using the triangle as a test of whether it will work. When you have a couple of outlines, show them to someone else, and talk about them. Get them to see if they can find any weak points in them. (You can probably do the same for them.)

(3) Try writing a full story from one of the diagrams given below – or if you prefer, from your own diagram from the previous exercise.

(a)

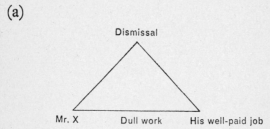

(Deciding factor not luck, but result of his lack of interest.)

(b)

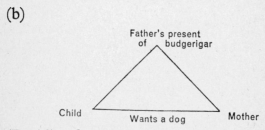

(Deciding factor could seem lucky, unless father is part of the story all the way through.)

(4) Exchange the finished stories with other people in the class. Get them to tell you:

(a) The best parts,

(b) The worst parts.

Then, in future, try to develop your use of the good points and so push out the bad ones.

This criticism is very valuable; try to get as much of it as you can.

2 Description

WE ought now, having settled the main plan of a story, to look at the question of the background against which the story will take place. The main story will need to be supported by a good background if the reader is going to really enter into it. As proof of this, try to imagine what it would be like to see a film in which all the action took place in front of a blank wall. If people in the story are going to a restaurant, then the reader wants to be able to picture them there, just as in a film your eyes would take in the background of tables, chairs, other diners and so on. Perhaps it will be useful to see just how this must be shown to the reader.

You have an idea of a scene in your mind: try to get it into as sharp focus as possible. If you look back at my description of a restaurant, you will see that it is "out of focus" – you cannot really get a clear picture at all – it might be any restaurant, anywhere. Once you have the picture clear in your own mind, then it must be transferred to the reader by your words so that he gets exactly the same picture.

Any idea must be really clear to you before you can hope to make it clear to your reader.

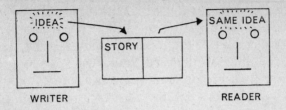

WRITER   READER

Here is a description from Walter Scott's *Ivanhoe*.
He is giving us a picture of the field on which a tour-
nament between knights is going to take place. Just as
if he were the camera in a film, Scott is looking round
and telling us exactly what he sees.

> On the verge of a wood which approaches to within a
> mile of the town of Ashby, was an extensive meadow, of
> the finest and most beautiful green turf, surrounded on
> one side by the forest, and fringed on the other by strag-
> gling oak-trees, some of which had grown to an immense
> size. The ground, as if fashioned on purpose for the
> martial display which was intended, sloped gradually
> down on all sides to a level bottom, which was enclosed
> for the lists with strong palisades, forming a space of a
> mile in length and about half as broad. The form of the
> enclosure was an oblong square, save that the corners
> were considerably rounded off, in order to afford more
> convenience for the spectators. The openings for the
> entry of the combatants were at the northern and south-
> ern extremities of the lists, accessible by strong wooden
> gates, each wide enough to admit two horsemen riding
> abreast.

And Scott goes on with this detailed description
for another five paragraphs. Certainly he had the
scene well drawn out in his mind. It is precise enough
for us to draw a map from it, including compass
directions.

However, for our purposes, the method has certain

disadvantages. For a start, Scott was writing a long novel, and writing it, too, in days when people had plenty of time to sit and read for hours at a time. To put it bluntly, we may all think that such long descriptive passages are just plain dull. In the shorter length of a short story, we must try to liven things up by doing more than just giving a word photograph of the scene.

One very simple device to remember here is that *nouns* are most effective in making a scene clear. Although adjectives are often referred to as describing words, they are far less useful at creating a really clear picture. Try it out:

White, dainty, green, solid, expensive.

With nouns the picture comes clearer:

Tablecloth, waitress, soup-bowl, chair, chandelier. The two together are even better:

White tablecloth, dainty waitress, green soup-bowl, and so on. The second point is that it is far better to use *singular nouns* than plural ones.

You can imagine a *girl* and add lots of extra description:

Fat, smiling, blonde, pink bow in her hair. You cannot do this with the word *girls*.

Singular nouns are the most effective basic words for building a scene.

Your own idea of a scene will have been formed by your own five senses . . . sight, hearing, smell, taste and touch. Even a film has a sound track and in the film shot of a restaurant we would expect to hear people walking about, chatting, and perhaps the chinking of plates. But in writing we can go three steps better and bring in the senses of touch, and less importantly, smell and taste. If we can put these ideas into the reader's mind, then he will feel, as nearly as possible, that he is really there – in the story with the characters.

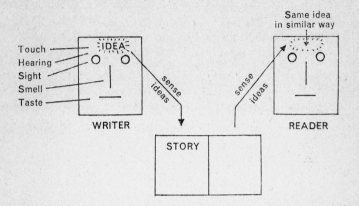

When John Trenchard, the hero of Meade Faulkner's novel, *Moonfleet*, is trapped in a vault under the village church, with only the coffins and the smugglers' barrels for company, the story is interwoven with the description like this:

> Here was another surprise, and a sad one for me, for I perceived that I had slept away a day, and that the sun was setting for another night. And yet it mattered little, for night or day time there was no light to help me in this horrible place; and although my eyes grew accustomed to the gloom I could make out nothing to show me where to work. So I took out my tinder-box meaning to fan the match into a flame and at least get one moment's look at the place, and then to set digging with my hands. But as I lay asleep the top had been pressed off the box and the salt damps had soddened it in the night, and spark by spark fell idle from the flint.
> And then it was I perceived the danger in which I

stood; for there was no hope of kindling a light and I doubted now whether even in the light I could ever have done much to dislodge the great slab of slate. I began also to feel very hungry, as not having eaten for twenty-four hours; and worse than that, there was a parching thirst and dryness in my throat and nothing with which to quench it. Yet there was no time to be lost if I was ever to get out alive, and so I groped with my hands against the side of the grave until I made out the bottom edge of the slab and then fell to grubbing beneath it with my fingers. But the earth which the day before had looked light and loamy to the eye, was stiff and hard when one came to tackle it with naked hands, and in an hour's time I had done little more than further weary myself and bruise my fingers.

Then I was forced to rest . . . but afterwards stood up and cried aloud . . . but there came no answer, except the echo of my own voice sounding hollow and far off down the vault.

A maddening thirst had hold of me. And then I thought of the barrels piled high in the vault and of the liquor that they held. Thus I groped my way about till near the top of the stack my hand struck on the spile of a barrel, and drawing it, I got my mouth to the hole. What the liquor was I do not know, but it was not so strong but that I could swallow it in great gulps and found it less burning than my burning throat. . . .

Here we can find every sense represented. Sight turns up in the opening sentence, and we are told that there is little light, which is why the passage relies so much on the other senses. Touch comes with the fumbling for the tinder, and the digging. There is a hint of smell in the phrase "salt damps" – we can imagine the odour of a sea-cave easily from that. Sound comes with his voice, and the echoes of it. Lastly, the little-used taste sense comes in with the liquor from the barrels.

A description that appeals to more than just the sense of sight will be far more vivid to the reader.

It is worth noting, too, that in the second sentence Faulkner refers not to "*that* horrible place" as we might expect, but to "*this* horrible place" – which again helps us to feel we are actually there with John Trenchard.

Although I have been emphasising the descriptive elements of this passage, you will note that it is telling quite a bit of the story, too – and that there is conflict between John and the vault. The description is doing more than one thing at a time, unlike the extract from Ivanhoe.

A description that is interwoven with the story is more interesting than one that is purely scene-setting.

Similarly, it is often possible to give more than a simple description by setting an overall mood to the passage. To go back to the restaurant again: we might make it a very busy one, where all the words would contrive to create a sensation of hustle and bustle. It might be a quiet one, when the waiters were idling lazily, or playing cards on one of the tables before the rush to come. Or an extremely unappetising place, and the general grubbiness and poor quality food might make the reader feel slightly sick – then we would be certain that he felt he was really there!

Charles Dickens is an expert on unpleasant scenes: here he is describing the way up to an attic, in his novel, *A Tale of Two Cities*, set at the time of the French Revolution:

Such a staircase with its accessories, in the older and more crowded parts of Paris, would be bad enough now;

27

but at any time, it was vile indeed to unaccustomed and unhardened senses. Every little habitation within the great foul nest of one high building . . . left its own heap of refuse on its own landing, besides flinging other refuse from its own windows. The uncontrollable and hopeless mass of decomposition so engendered, would have polluted the air, even if poverty and deprivation had not loaded it with their intangible impurities. . . .

The smell of poverty is obvious! Out of the simple act of one character walking up the stairs we have a picture of the whole area and its mood.

A description must be more than a set of precise details: it should have its own mood, or emotion, and be part of the story as well.

One of the easiest ways of contriving all these things at once is to describe the background of the story as seen and felt by the central character. This is an excellent device since:

(a) It sets the scene for the reader.

(b) It tells the reader about the characters and their feelings.

(c) It keeps the story going.

(d) By having one central idea, it keeps the details from falling apart into a jumbled list of random ideas.

Perhaps most important of all, it encourages the readers to put themselves into the story – they feel they are the hero or heroine, and once they have done this it is easy to hold their attention.

No doubt you have felt this involvement at some time, when reading a book or watching a film or television play. You are anxious when the hero is in danger: you are miserable when the heroine loses her boy-friend: you hope that the villain will not get away. Once you are caught up in the story like this, your interest is held for good. In descriptive paragraphs, where it is easy to lose hold on the reader, the more you can help them to get involved in this way, the better.

Involvement can be helped by a personal bias in the description, as well as by appealing to all the senses.

I want to end this section with a passage written by Anne Frank. She was a Jewess living in Holland during the last War, and she and her family had to go into hiding to avoid being caught by the Germans, who were imprisoning all Jews at the time. Here she is describing the "Secret Annexe" in which they were to spend two years.

> The Secret Annexe is an ideal hiding-place. Although it leans to one side and is damp, you'd never find such a comfortable hiding-place anywhere in Amsterdam; no, perhaps not even in the whole of Holland. Our little room looked very bare at first with nothing on the walls; but thanks to Daddy who had brought my film-star collection and picture post-cards on beforehand, and with the aid of paste-pot and brush, I have transformed the walls into one gigantic picture. This makes it look more cheerful, and, when the Van Daans come, we'll get some wood from the attic, and make a few little cupboards for the walls and other odds and ends to make it more lively. . . .
>
> We made some curtains straight away on the first day. Really one can hardly call them curtains, they are just light, loose strips of material all different shapes, which Daddy and I sewed together in a most unprofessional way. The works of art are fixed in position with drawing pins, not to come down until we emerge from here.

This is a very effective piece of writing, although it is done in the simplest phrases. Anne Frank was only thirteen when she wrote this passage in her diary.

The use of detail is clear enough: there is no complete description of the room – instead we hear about the film-star collection, the curtains, the plans for the cupboards. We feel because of this that we can picture the whole room – we are led to invent in our minds what is obvious and unimportant – four walls, the door, chairs and so on.

The sense of sight is used in the main, with a little appeal to the sense of touch in the mention of dampness.

The mood is cheerful – and it is this that holds our interest, because the reason for using the Annexe was depressing enough. When Anne left there, it was to go to a prison-camp where she died. Nevertheless we are made to feel the excitement of making a home in an unlikely place, and the fun that could be had out of the whole situation. We are invited to share her amusement at the clumsy results of their sewing – particularly by the teasing reference to them as "works of art".

Already something of Anne's character is showing – cheerfulness, even under terrifying circumstances. In the next section we will discuss this matter of putting characters into the settings.

Assignment 2

(a) Try actually drawing a map from Sir Walter Scott's description.

(b) Find a map in an atlas, and imagine yourself somewhere on it, where you would get a good view. Then describe what you see – when you're not sure, just invent.

(c) Settle on a mood for a description and try to describe any scene with this mood in mind. (Choose from one of these suggestions only if you can't think of one of your own.) Moods: dampness, gaiety, brightness, noisiness, coldness, peace, terror. Scenes: a cave, a river, a zoo, a classroom, a deserted house, a forest.

(d) Try to describe what it would be like for a blind person to stand beside the sea. (Since we so often overdo the sense of sight, it is very interesting to see just how realistic a scene can be done in this way. In addition you will have a ready-made personal bias.)

(e) Would you now check the number of words that you usually get to one page of writing. People's writing varies a lot in size, but your own will probably not vary by more than twenty words to the page. There are two reasons for getting you to do this: firstly, it is much easier for me to suggest lengths in number of words than in number of pages; secondly, it is usually reckoned that ten words to the minute is a reasonable writing speed in an examination – i.e. an hour's work gives six hundred words.

Having done that, see how effective a description you can do – of any subject that you like – in about one hundred words. (Don't count them; you can guess it to half a page, two thirds of a page, etc.)

(f) Now take the description you have just done and try to squeeze it down to half its original length, losing as little as possible of the effect in the process.

3 Characters

NOTE: Much of this section, by the way, may be useful to you in reverse, when you are asked to do a "character sketch" of a person from someone else's story or play. Instead of building a person, as you do in your own writing, you take them apart.

HAVING decided on a story-line, or plot, and decided also on the background setting for it, and the ways in which we shall sketch this in, we need to start work on the characters involved.

Some of the characters will have already been decided by the plot itself – the conflict may arise between two farmers in a quarrel over a piece of land, for instance. But so far, they will only be names, not real people. We have to expand the ideas and try to get the puppets to come alive.

One trap which is only too easy to fall into is to have too many characters. A novel of sixty thousand words may have only four or five main characters: so in six hundred words we must limit the number of characters severely. A single person is perfectly possible – but it makes it difficult to include any conversation, which is one of the best ways of bringing a character alive. Two people are better; three, about the most we can hope to use.

Keep down the number of characters.

Another problem that often crops up is that, when you have, for example, three men, it is very awkward to use "he". We cannot be sure who is meant each time. An easy way round this is to start with perhaps two men and a woman and to write the story as if you were one of the men – that way we have "I", "he", and "she". We also have a variety of people, which makes the job much easier all round.

Writing in the first person is a very valuable device.

Whenever you do write in the first person, remember that you do not have to write as yourself – you can make yourself into any character you want. Nor need you be young – you can be five, or ninety-five. You can even try changing your sex – which often makes for an interesting story, although it is difficult to do well.[1]

First decide on the number of essential characters and the view point from which you are going to write.

We saw that any story is a selection of likely events – not just any events – and character planning is just the same. We need to select some part of the person's character to emphasise. The key to which part is the word *motive*. These people will be doing things in the story – why do they do them, and not something else? Once this question is answered – it may be greed, or hatred, or love, or stupidity – then we know what part we must emphasise. It is most important

[1] In *The Professor* Charlotte Brontë writes as a man; in *Moll Flanders* Daniel Defoe writes as a woman.

to see that it is the inside of the person that matters – not what they look like.

We never know a person completely from a photograph: we have to speak to them, to see what they do, before we know much about them. It is the same in a story: you must show the reader the inside of the person, not just the outside.

There are five ways in which character can be demonstrated: what they look like, what they do, what they say, what they think, and what people say about them.

Here are some extracts from Jane Austen's book *Pride and Prejudice* in which she is telling us about Mr. Darcy, one of the two main characters.

> . . . Mr. Darcy soon drew the attention of the room by his fine, tall person, handsome features, noble mien and the report which was in general circulation within five minutes after his entrance, of his having ten thousand a year. The gentlemen pronounced him to be a fine figure of a man, the ladies declared he was much handsomer than Mr. Bingley and he was looked at with great admiration. . . .

Here we have a combination of what is said about him, and what he actually looks like, and it is the comment on him that is of greatest interest. There is a bias in the description, too: his wealth adds greatly to his attractiveness.

However, Mr. Darcy is soon shown acting and speaking. Neither he nor the heroine is dancing at the time, and Darcy's friend suggests he might like to dance with someone, for example, Elizabeth.

Darcy's reply is:

> "Which do you mean?" and turning round he looked for a moment at Elizabeth, till catching her eye, he withdrew his own and coldly said:

> "She is tolerable, but not handsome enough to tempt *me*; and I am in no humour at present to give consequence to young ladies who are slighted by other men."

At once we have a new impression of him: so do the other people at the ball.

> ... He was discovered to be proud, to be above his company, and above being pleased; and not all his large estate in Derbyshire could stop him from having a most forbidding and disagreeable countenance. ...

We are aware that their opinion of his looks has altered – he actually looks different to them now that he has insulted Elizabeth; which demonstrates just how unimportant looks are.

What does he think? Here we have another surprise. We would expect that he has a poor opinion of Elizabeth, but we find, in fact, that he was ill at ease at the ball, that he does not like dancing much, and his opinion of Elizabeth is altering as he sees more of her:

> ... But no sooner had he made it clear to himself and his friends that she had hardly a good feature in her face, than he began to find it was rendered uncommonly intelligent by the beautiful expression of her dark eyes. ...

Mr. Darcy, in fact, is falling in love with Elizabeth – to his own surprise, and even more to hers. The rest of the story concerns the resolving of this conflict between Mr. Darcy and Elizabeth.

Characters can alter as the story progresses, as long as the alteration is not sudden or unreal.

Frequently the change brought about in someone's character by the conflict in the story adds greatly to its interest. When people are in difficult situations, the most interesting things can happen to their normal characters – the coward may suddenly show that he has bravery we did not expect; the pleasant people show their hidden spitefulness; the hard-hearted ones may be human after all.

So long as the reader is convinced that there is a good enough reason for this change of character, and so long as he feels he is getting to know more about the person all the time, he will remain interested.

Minor characters need sketching in quickly with as few words as possible.

Again Jane Austen can show us some good ideas: here are two comments on Mary Bennett, one of Elizabeth's sisters:

> . . . the only plain one in the family . . .
> . . . Mary wished to say something sensible, but knew not how.

In two phrases Mary is depicted as stupid and plain. When she starts trying to entertain guests by playing badly on the piano, and fails to realise that their praise is polite, not genuine, we have a neat, accurate picture of her – through her actions, her words, and a little straight description.

Characters should be few in number. The main ones can be introduced slowly to the reader, so that he gets to know them as if he has met them, the minor ones should be quickly dealt with.

It is through the characters that the conflict develops, of course. Often the conflict will depend on the clash of personalities involved. This is good: but it tends to make people think that characters should always be arguing.

To have an argument in which the sides are evenly balanced is almost pointless. No one has any chance of winning. Conflict is always more interesting when it is between characters who are unevenly matched, as were Elizabeth and Mr. Darcy. He appears to have all the advantages in the scene; naturally we hope that Elizabeth will have her revenge – on another occasion, she will be in the winning position. So the action develops with the reader continually interested. A drawn match is less satisfactory.

We shall look more closely at the whole subject of conversation in the next section, but one fascinating thing about building a character is that, if you have laid the basic plan and can really imagine them as real people, they will have a life of their own in your mind, and will start telling you what to put down. You know just what they will do, or say, at any time. Once they have come alive like this for you, you can be sure that they will have done so for the reader.

So far, we have looked at plot, background and characters, and it may be useful to see just how much we can plan out beforehand, before writing the first line of a story. You may not like to plan this much on paper, preferring to "let the story come" as you write; there is nothing wrong with doing this, and eventually you should be able to do it all in your head, but I would strongly advise you to put as much plan as possible down on paper to start with. You can waste so much time in trying to write a story that has something badly wrong with its plan, that it would never "come right". As a guide, you might reckon that half your time wants to be spent on the planning at first. Moreover, you will find it much more interesting to have the story running round in your mind and be able to put it straight down, than to be continually getting stuck and spending most of your time sucking your pencil and gazing at the ceiling.

Assignment 3

(a) Write three brief character sketches, two as normal prose, the other as part of a conversation, each not longer than twenty-five words.

(b) In about seventy words, give a realistic indication of character, using all the devices discussed.

(c) Re-write the above in the first person, trying to give the reader exactly the same indication of character.

(d) Try analysing your own character, and introduce yourself into a story as one of the characters (about three hundred words).

(e) You are now free to write a story – suggested length of five hundred to six hundred words – trying to introduce as many of the points dealt with in the first three sections as you find useful. Do not strain to put them in – let the story come naturally; afterwards look back and see how much you have relied on the ideas from the book. If you are already using these ideas without noticing it, you are doing well.

4 Dialogue

WHY should conversation be such an important part of a story? I think it helps to see what happens if you cut out all the rest of story-telling and leave only the conversation – you end up with a play. In a play, the characters come alive to a far greater extent than they can in a story, since there are actors to play the parts, but good conversation will encourage the reader to see the whole thing enacted in his mind's eye, or imagination – and once again remember that if the story comes alive, then it will be enjoyed.

There are two principal ways of putting conversation in: we may either give the actual words, as in the play, or we may abbreviate them and merely say roughly what was said. The first is known as "direct speech", the second as "indirect".

Direct speech gives the best impression of character, and is the more dramatic form.

In this passage from *The Small Back Room* by Nigel Balchin, Sammy Rice is on the telephone to Stuart. They are both experts in bomb disposal, and have been trying to solve the problem of dismantling an enemy booby-trap. Previously all they had been able to find were the remains of the bombs, and of the people who had been killed trying to pick them up:

It was Stuart. He said, "I've got one, old boy."

I said, "My God, have you? In one piece?"

"Yes. In fact, I've got two. Complete, undamaged and in mint condition."

"Where?"

"I'm at Luganporth. They're down on the sands about two miles away. I've got cordons round them."

"On the sands?"

"Yes. Couldn't be better, could it? I think they must have been jettisoned."

I said, "You've seen them?"

"Yes, I've taken a fairly respectful look."

"Like we thought?"

"Fairly. Bit bigger. We were a hundred per cent wrong about one thing though."

"What?"

Stuart said, "Tick-tock, tick-tock."

"Time?"

"Apparently."

"Are you sure?"

"Oh, yes. I heard it myself. Look, old boy – I take it you want to be in on this? You don't have to, of course, but . . ."

I said, "Of course I do."

"Right. Then this is the idea – I shall give them until tomorrow morning to do their stuff by themselves. Then, if they haven't, I shall have a go."

I said, "How early can I get down?"

"Wait a minute. As we've got two, the obvious thing is to try them in series. I'll have a go. Then if I make a pig's ear you'll know some of the things not to do with the other. Agree?"

"You'll wait till I get down?"

"Depends what time you arrive. But anyhow, I'll see that absolutely everything's recorded."

I thought for a moment and then said, "I'd much rather you waited till I got there."

40

"Why?" said Stuart. I heard him chuckle to himself. "Two heads are better than one."

"Yes. But we can't do a joint thing, old boy. Otherwise if it goes wrong there won't be anyone to cope with the other one."

Much of the conversation here seems to be telling us facts: that two unexploded bombs have been dropped, that they are apparently time-bombs, and that Sammy will travel down to help. But more than this we have an impression of two very different characters: Stuart, looking on the whole thing like a game, which he is out to win. Only the remark about "If I make a pig's ear . . ." shows that he does appreciate he may be killed. In fact his light tone is part of a defence against the danger.

Sammy is older and more serious; anxious that he should be there to help – although it is not his assignment. Some of the background is filled in by the caution they take over the 'phone call: to anyone overhearing it would mean little – "tick-tock", "I've got two", "I'll have a go".

Where it is merely necessary to put over information then we can use indirect speech, which is shorter, but less interesting.

Stuart rang me up and told me he had found two of the bombs. We discussed them briefly, and I arranged to join him in Luganporth.

This would tell us nothing about character: it has no dramatic interest. Nevertheless, when it is only a matter of explaining that there was a conversation, it is sufficient and takes up less space.

Often a mixture of both methods works well, the parts of the conversation that are picked out for the direct treatment giving enough indication of character.

The most obvious methods of conversation can be varied on occasions. For example, with a telephone conversation, we may give only the one side, and let the reader guess at the rest. The usual way of showing this is to indicate the pauses by rows of dots.

> ". . . Hullo. John? . . . Oh, yes, fine. And you? . . . Good. What I wanted to know was whether you've got a French dictionary I could borrow for the evening . . . Yes, homework! . . . Of course, I'll take care of it . . . Oh, but that was an accident. . . ."

The little hint of conflict keeps the interest going: it appears that John is not too keen to lend the book after what happened last time. All the usual preliminaries can be cut to half-length this way, too.

With one hand over the mouthpiece, it is easy to get thoughts spoken aloud to another person, too: the nearest thing to a Shakespearean aside.

> ". . . See if you can find it then . . ." Mike turned to his sister: "He nearly wouldn't lend it to me; just because he's hoping to get top marks in that French test, too, I bet . . . John? Thanks a lot. I'll come over and pick it up. . . ."

Although conversation is so useful it has certain difficulties.

It is worth realising that punctuation of direct speech is much more difficult than that of ordinary prose. The big disadvantage is that until you are able to put in all the inverted commas and commas from force of habit, you can spend too much time wondering how to get it right, instead of thinking of what you want to say.

One way is to put down in rough just what your characters are saying without worrying about punctuation at all, and then copy it up adding punctuation as you go – but this is still a time-wasting business. Often people do not realise just how short actual sentences are in speech. Look how many one word sentences there are in the extract above. Words like "yes", "no", "fine", often have a whole sentence to themselves. And most essential, you must change paragraphs whenever the speaker changes.

The best test of whether the speech is good, is to read it aloud. Have you given someone an impossible sentence to say, like: "I do not think that I shall be able to come but if, however, I find that time permits, then I shall do so." This is perfectly correct English, but terrible conversation! "I don't think that I can make it. Look – if I can I will, but I can't be sure."

See how it is much more broken up, and note the use of "don't" and "can't". Usually we avoid these abbreviated forms in writing unless they are inside inverted commas, but in speech we nearly always run words together in this way, and not to do so in a story makes it sound unreal. Of course, it just makes punctuation more difficult again.

Another thing to avoid is the use of someone who speaks bad English – a character who drops "h's", or uses slang continually. This is a clumsy piece of character building, and requires doing extremely well to be effective. More often it just sounds like a bad piece of writing.

Speech must sound natural when read aloud, should add to character, but not hold up the story. When it starts to do so, switch to indirect speech.

Apart from the advice to try for a natural sound, and to listen for what your characters would really say in those circumstances – rather than "making" them say something, there is not a lot to add. Speech stems from having a clear idea of the character in your mind: if you have that, then what they say will demonstrate character effectively.

However, the exact way in which they say it is sometimes not easy to put down. "I don't want to do that," "I don't want to do that," and "I don't want to do that" all mean something slightly different. Underlining in this way is a simple and effective trick: but rather obvious. Neater and more subtle, is to break the speech just after the word you want to emphasise by a phrase like, "he said".

"You can do it," he said – and "You," he said, "can do it," each have slightly different emphasis.

Breaking speeches in this way avoids the monotony of a row of "he saids" all through the story. Better still, leave out the phrase where you can.

See how it is done in the extract from *The Small Back Room*, just an odd reminder who is speaking, and then we are allowed to guess.

Never forget just how powerful speech is in revealing character, even in a single remark.

Jane Hope has just entered a college, and wants to find someone to talk to. There is one other girl in the room:

> After several minutes I remarked tentatively: "My name is Hope."
> "Mine," she replied, "is not." (*Don't Do It!*)

In two lines we have a neat picture of the shy new girl, and the completely crushing superior attitude of one of the old-established members.

Direct and indirect thought are equally revealing and are the great advantage that a story has over a play.

44

When talking about characters, we saw that their speech and thoughts were two of the ways of expressing them. In a play, you can only hear what the people actually say. (Except by the now out-of-date method where the character spoke directly to the audience and told them what he was thinking. This was known as "soliloquy", and Shakespeare uses it to great effect, although it sounds artificial on the stage in a modern play.)

Here Macbeth is thinking aloud about whether he should murder Duncan the king, and so take the crown himself:

> ". . . He's here in double trust:
> First, as I am his kinsman and his subject,
> Strong both against the deed; then, as I am his host
> Who should against the murdered shut the door,
> Not bear the knife myself. . . ."

His mental struggle against temptation is an important part of his character, and also part of the story.

Again, in *Henry VI* (*Part One*) we find a neat mixture of speech and thinking aloud, that tells us a lot about Lord Somerset.

> All: (including Somerset) Welcome High Prince, the mighty Duke of York.
> Somerset: (thinking aloud) Perish base prince, ignoble Duke of York.

Setting speech and thought in contrast in this way can be very revealing, and it can easily be done in a story.

Direct speech and direct thought are punctuated in exactly the same way: "What a pleasure to meet you!" said Charles, thinking, "Who on earth is this idiot?"

A mixture of direct and indirect speech, and direct thought, provide endless opportunities for development of character.

The last extract is taken from *Quatermass and the Pit* by Nigel Kneale, and is part of a television script. Here it is the dialogue which is of supreme importance. It must tell the story, and show the characters. The camera directions correspond to the descriptive passages in the book.

Roney has been called in to a building site to investigate fossil remains of some apemen found there. His digging only serves to expose what is believed to be an unexploded bomb. Breen and Quatermass, both from the Ministry of Defence, have come to examine it:

> Cut to excavation floor, where the Sergeant has also noticed the figures moving above. He touches Potter's arm and nods towards the ramp. Potter glances round and goes quickly to meet the newcomers. Breen comes first.

POTTER (saluting): I'm in charge here, sir. Can I help you?

BREEN: That's rather the question *I* was going to ask.

RONEY (to Potter): This is Colonel Breen, of guided missiles. And Professor Quatermass.

> Potter stiffens.

BREEN (with a nod towards the hole): What have you got there?

POTTER: I – I don't know yet, sir.

BREEN: Informed your superiors?

POTTER (glowering at Roney): Not yet, sir.

BREEN: Mind if we take a look?

> He leads the way towards the trench-like hole. Seeing them coming, the Sergeant turns to the Sappers and mutters an order. They scramble clear.

46

Breen, Quatermass, and the others come down –
and stand staring.

Fade in music.

The thing in the trench is laid bare to a length of
about eight feet, a whale-backed shape, and clearly
indicating by its gentle curve the enormous bulk
that must still lie hidden underneath.

BREEN: A bomb?

POTTER (at Breen's side): There's been no sign of an in-
gress cavity, sir – I checked with the firm who did the
excavating.

BREEN: I suppose the hole might have collapsed . . .
closed up. . . .

Quatermass is glancing round.

QUATERMASS: The famous excavation.

RONEY: Yes. (Unhappily) We're probably standing on
priceless fossils at this moment.

QUATERMASS: Aha?

RONEY: About here they dug out the first skull.

Quatermass moves forward along the edge of the
trench. Breen follows, eyes on the thing below them.

QUATERMASS: A trifle muddy.

Breen slips and almost crashes down into the trench.
Quatermass puts out an arm and grabs him.

BREEN: Thanks –

They step up on to the firmer sandbags on the
other side. After a moment Quatermass calls across
to the others.

QUATERMASS: Roney – where did you say the skull was
found? Where *exactly*?

RONEY: In the earth that's all been dug away now. Two or
three feet above this level. (He turns to Barbara)
That's right, isn't it?

BARBARA: Yes, it *was* here.

QUATERMASS (sharply): You said *above*?

BREEN: What's wrong?

QUATERMASS: If it was above this thing – (He calls again).
Roney, tell me – how long did you estimate the skull
had been there?

RONEY: Something like . . . five million years.

QUATERMASS (a whisper): Five . . . million . . . years . . . !
>His eyes drop to the shape in the trench below.
>Track in quickly to close-up.
>Crash in end music.
>Fade vision to black.

Assignment 4

(a) 1 Write a brief conversation between two people, preferably with some conflict in it – i.e. an argument. (About one hundred and fifty words.)

2 Now take the least interesting part, and convert it into indirect speech.

3 Now add the thoughts of both characters especially where they differ from what they say (bringing it back to original length, or a bit more).

(b) 1 Try a full story of five hundred to six hundred words, using the new techniques described in this section.

2 Exchange stories and exercises, and check each other's punctuation – it might even be an idea to do a punctuation exercise, so that it will come automatically next time you write.

(c) 1 Listen carefully to a radio play, or the soundtrack of a television play, and see how close you think it is to real speech.

2 Write a one-minute conversation for radio – two characters – about one hundred and thirty words. Get it read aloud by two people, and see if it sounds natural (making allowances for whether they read it well, but the better it is written, the easier it will be for them to read, so do not put all the blame on them).

5 Ideas and Credibility

THERE are few more depressing things than to be faced with a blank sheet of paper, wishing to write something on it, and finding that your own mind seems as blank as the paper. So where do you go to find ideas?

Firstly, if you think about it, your mind never is really blank. Try hard to think about nothing, and you can soon prove that yourself. There are ideas racing around in your head all the time, and it is a matter of getting the usable ones, and putting them down on paper.

It is quite useless, too, to try looking for a completely new idea: no one has ever had one, not even the greatest inventors. What happens when you invent something, is that you take what you know and rearrange it: the result is what we call "new."

If an idea for a story were really, and absolutely, new, then you would have to invent entirely new words to tell it.

When James Watt invented a new device – the steam engine – it was the old idea of boiling water plus the old idea of a pump plus the old idea of blowing, which gave the completely new idea of steam blowing a pump to make a steam engine.

So all we need look for are new arrangements of old ideas. Shakespeare, by the way, borrowed most of his plots: from history books, old stories, or other people's plays. *Hamlet* had been around for some time before Shakespeare re-wrote it – and *West Side Story* is *Romeo and Juliet* in disguise. So we can cheerfully borrow from other people. By the time we have written it down, it should be so different that no one will know.

With backgrounds there are various possibilities. You can simply use those you know – school, home, your own town – or you can use ones of which you have no personal experience, but of which you know enough to make them convincing. It is sometimes said that you can only write about what you yourself have experienced. On the face of it, this must be non-sense. Daniel Defoe was never marooned on a desert island, yet he created a convincing picture of this in *Robinson Crusoe*. He had, however, talked with a sailor who had been marooned, and from these con-versations gained the ideas needed for the book.

There is nothing wrong with "second-hand" ideas. Every major writer has used them.

You must have some real basis for your writing though. You cannot write about piloting an aircraft unless you have, for example, read some auto-biographies of pilots, or some fiction on the subject, or seen several flying films.

Since the ideas from there will be passed on to you, you can in turn, by your imagination, create again the feeling of flying an aeroplane. You may well know more about it this way, than by being a passenger in aircraft twice a week. So long as you do not try to invent too far, so that it becomes obvious that you are "only making it up", then it should be convincing.

Pictures of foreign countries from travel brochures, plus a few details from a geography book, can give you sufficient information to set your scene in Egypt or Scandinavia. If you have ever been abroad, then try to reconstruct the scenery sufficiently to give the story a fresh slant.

Remember that it is details that are important – not vague outlines; so that a few green dates hanging from a palm-tree beside a gritty and smelly pool in the desert will be quite enough to bring Egypt to the reader's mind – he has probably never been there either.

With characters, too, you can start from people you know – school-friends (and enemies), your parents, your relations – and then mix them up. What would your Aunt Maud have been like as a girl of eight? What will you be like when you are running your own business with a hundred workers under you? What is it you dislike about young Algernon, and would it be sufficient motive for a murder?

What you must beware of, is taking all the ideas from one place: particularly from a book or a film. This is stealing rather than borrowing, and you will only end up with a second-hand, second-rate version of a story that everyone has heard before.

The whole point of imagination is re-organising ideas, mixing them up, altering them, juggling them to suit your story.

Start from what you know, but add to it and alter it as much as you can.

How do you work? There are as many answers as

writers, but here are some views, first from *The End of the Affair* by Graham Greene:

> One may be preoccupied with shopping and income tax returns and chance conversations, but the stream of the unconscious continues to flow undisturbed, solving problems, planning ahead: one sits down sterile and dispirited at the desk, and suddenly the words come as through the air; the situations that seemed blocked in a hopeless impasse move forward; the work has been done while one slept or shopped or talked with friends. . . .

This is very useful advice, in that it is often helpful to let your ideas run through your mind for as long as possible before you actually have to write:

> Over twenty years I have probably averaged five hundred words a day for five days a week. I can produce a novel in a year, and that allows time for revision and the correction of the typescript. I have always been methodical and when my quota of work is done, I break off even in the middle of a scene. . . .

So you can see it is not a bad thing to *have* to do some writing as homework, with a set time for handing it in. Like a novelist or a reporter, you have a deadline, and must keep to it. Too often, if we do not have one, it is easy never to write anything – just because you are never quite "in the mood".

This idea that you cannot write unless you feel like doing so is very widespread: nevertheless I think it is unsound. Certainly there are times when you feel "inspired" and times when you seem to have no ideas, or you cannot put them down to your satisfaction.

The only way to make the former more frequent and the latter even less, does seem to be to force yourself to write, even if you know it to be poor stuff.

No footballer would stop practising because he was shooting wide of the goal: this is just the time when he needs to practise more. Since both footballers and writers have this in common – that they are trying to improve their skill – I think that the same rule applies. One might make an exception for the most experienced players and writers: not for those who are apprentices.

Here are some other views – I would not agree with all of them, but they all come from people who are keenly interested in writing.

Boy age thirteen:

I get a lot of ideas from films and television. Then I try to use the themes in places I know – Scouts and school mostly. I put a lot of notes down first, and then usually tear them up and write from memory.

Boy age fifteen:

Writing is hard work and I don't really enjoy it until it's finished. When I read it, it often seems as if I hadn't written it at all, I like to write as fast as I can, and then tidy it up at the end. I think you get a more flowing story that way.

Boy age eleven:

I do my essay as my last bit of homework, because that way the ideas seem to sort out for you better. I don't make any notes. I get my main character in a mess, and then see how I can get him out. I don't like writing about girls.

Girl age thirteen:

Most of the time I don't like what I write, and I'm always tearing it up. I do a lot of rough work, but not working out notes. I just don't seem to be able to write that way. I get a lot of ideas when I'm in the bath.

Girl age thirteen:

I don't see how you can write unless you feel you want to. You cannot just think up a story because someone – usually a teacher – says you must. I do my best stories in the holidays, and try to use them up as homework if we don't have a set title.

Girl age fifteen:

I think it is preferable to have a set title, since this channels your thoughts towards a definite end. I used to plan stories in detail with character outlines, but now I find I can do without this. I suppose it was good practice, though. My great weakness is in dialogue writing at the moment, and I try to avoid much conversation. I like writing in the first person, since I can let my imagination have free rein (I suppose that's a cliché), and be anyone I choose.

Boy age twelve:

No one has mentioned reading. I don't see how you can learn much about writing if you don't see how the good people do it. I think you want a library ticket to be able to write.

Girl age fourteen:

If you have a good ending, then you get a good story. I like to start with an ending and work back from that.

All of which shows how varied the views can be. Your own way may be as different again. If you have not yet acquired a real method of working, I would recommend: Make yourself write – it can never do you any harm. Use notes in as much detail as you can bear: as you grow more experienced, you will find you need them less. Spend plenty of thinking-time beforehand. Read as much as you can.

Once we have collected ideas, though, we have to convince the readers that we are telling the truth. Although they will know that the whole story is invented, while they are actually reading it they must believe it, and feel themselves part of it. This is sometimes known as the "suspension of disbelief" – the readers agree to believe in the story so that they can enjoy it. Unfortunately, it is only too easy to jolt them out of this willing agreement to the point where they say: "Oh, it's only a story – it doesn't even sound true." This we must clearly avoid.

To begin with, there are various themes which by their nature are asking for trouble. Stories set in the future are one example: often science fiction. The reader knows perfectly well that people from other planets have not come here in flying saucers, and to tell them so invites disbelief.

Obviously it can be done – has been done often, and much less frequently, well. The best science fiction has been written though, by scientists, or those with a very good knowledge of science.

In this extract Fred Hoyle, an eminent astronomer, who writes science fiction for fun, finds an unusual way of asking us to believe him.

The Black Cloud, which gives the book its title, has come to the solar system causing a great many problems – among them, cutting off the sunlight, and nearly freezing the earth completely:

> In many parts of the tropics and semi-tropics, as many as one person in two lost his life. Among the Esquimaux there was comparatively little loss.

In addition, it puzzles the astronomers observing it, because it does not seem to obey the accepted scientific laws.

Kingsley, one of the scientists, offers a startling explanation, which no reader is going to accept easily even if he has been convinced of the coming of the cloud itself:

"Without frills, what exactly do you mean, Chris?" someone asked.

"I mean that the cloud contains an intelligence. Before anyone starts criticising, let me say I know it's a preposterous idea, and I wouldn't suggest it for a moment if the alternative weren't even more outrageously preposterous. Doesn't it strike you how often we've been wrong about the behaviour of the cloud?"

Parkinson and Ann Halsey exchanged an amused glance.

"All our mistakes have a certain hallmark about them. They're just the sort of mistake that it'd be natural to make if, instead of the cloud being inanimate, it were alive. . . ."

His first bald statement was greeted with outright disbelief, even by his fellow scientists – Alexandrov excepted.

Weichart was frank in his opinion.

"The whole idea is quite ridiculous," he said.

Marlowe shook his head.

"This comes of reading science fiction. . . ."

By making some of the characters just as disbelieving as the readers, Hoyle is able to convince the readers as the other scientists become convinced themselves – as, of course, they do. The remark about science fiction is brilliant – by sneering at science fiction like this, Hoyle convinces his readers that this scene must be taking place in science fact.

Another theme that is superficially attractive, but far too difficult to attempt without a great deal of thought, is the supernatural. Ghosts are fascinating creatures; the snag is that not many people believe in them: they need persuasion. If you must try a ghost story, then beware of overdoing the effect. The whole point of ghosts is that they are mysterious, and to give too many exact details is, for once, a disadvantage.

The white-hooded figure, carrying clanking chains and its head under its arm, is more of a joke than convincing. The candle that is blown out by a soft breeze is more credible. But when there is no wind outside, it is subtly horrifying.

The unknown is always more sinister than what is explained.

Clumsy choices of first persons create almost impossible problems. I have seen "*My Story, by a puppy*" suggested as a title in a school text-book! I can imagine major novelists refusing to attempt such a task. Children of five are prepared to accept talking animals and fairies – but we are setting out to interest ourselves, not five-year-olds.

Much the same problems – worse, if anything – apply to stories allegedly told by things, instead of people. They are rarely convincing. In any case, why make the job more difficult than it is already?

"*A Day in the Life of a Penny*" – when you have written it, will it be worth reading? It is practically doomed from the start.

There are tremendous possibilities for your central character, so it is unnecessary and unwise to use anything other than people.

In the general adventure story like *King Solomon's Mines* it is still important that the reader shall be convinced, as soon as possible, of the absolute truth of it. Rider Haggard therefore spent two pages of preface giving some intentionally dull, and very detailed "facts" about the flowers and animals of the area, and "signed" it with the name of the central character, ending like this:

> ... And now it only remains for me to offer apologies for my blunt way of writing. I can but say in excuse of it that I am more accustomed to handle a rifle than a pen, and cannot make any pretence to the grand literary flights and flourishes which I see in novels – for sometimes I like to read a novel. I suppose they – the flights and flourishes – are desirable, and regret not being able to supply them. At the same time, I cannot help thinking that simple things are easier to understand when – like the Bible – they are written in plain language, though perhaps I have no right to set up an opinion on such a matter. "A sharp spear," runs the Kukana saying, "needs no polish," and on that principle I venture to hope that a true story, however strange it may be, does not require to be decked out in fine words.
>
> ALLAN QUARTERMAIN.

Although we have not space in a short story for such detail, it is worth studying this technique since we must attempt to do the same thing, with much greater economy.

A few really detailed references are a help; more important, anything suspicious must be avoided. Far too often people will give a completely impossible "fact" – a ridiculously high speed for a car, low cost for a painting, height of a mountain. As soon as this has happened, the reader's belief is destroyed.

Beware of impossibilities.

Assignment 5
(a) Take a story that you know well, or an incident that has actually happened to you, or a report from the newspaper. Then try altering it so as to make it

58

really your own, and write it in full to about six hundred words.

(b) See how far you can really create a frightening ghostly atmosphere, or the atmosphere of a foreign country. A geography book will make a useful source of background information here.

(c) Write a preface for a science fiction novel of about one hundred and fifty words.

(d) Write a simple, invented story, which anyone will take to be actually true. Use yourself as you really are, as the central character.

6 Openings, Middles and Endings

IT is in openings and endings that the differences between the short story and the novel show up most clearly. Although we have already seen that the whole story must work on a much simpler framework, because it is so much shorter – must have a simpler plot, fewer characters – the start and finish points are where the short story has a technique all of its own.

OPENINGS

Whatever you do when planning your story, never expect to be able to write an introduction. In a book of six hundred pages there may be room for something of this type, but in a story of six hundred words there is no room at all.

The first sentence must take us directly into the story.

Although it seems at first that you cannot expect a reader to follow the story unless you tell him first where it is happening, and who the characters are, this is in actual fact unnecessary.

A couple of thousand years ago Roman writers were saying just this in three neat words: "*In medias res*" – "In the middle of the thing" – and that is where the story should start.

Think through what will happen in the course of your story, and find the first really exciting part. Start there. As you write on you can fill in the background details quite naturally, letting the reader pick up the information as he goes.

This has two effects. First, the opening is really interesting. This attracts the reader, and invites him to read on. Second, he does not yet really know what the whole story is about – another reason why he should go on reading.

A novelist has a different problem: anyone who has a long book in his hand is much more prepared to work his way through a slow opening than a reader who has only a page or two of writing which he can either read or not. Nevertheless, you have probably suffered from the book where "nothing has happened" at the end of the first chapter.

Start in the middle of the story. Let the background fill in as you go.

For some examples of this, you can look at the stories at the end of this book.

Conversation makes an ideal opening, since it introduces us to one of the characters at once. Here is H. G. Wells's opening to his short story *In The Abyss*:

> The lieutenant stood in front of the steel sphere and gnawed a piece of pine splinter.
> "What do you think of it, Steevens?" he asked.
> "It's an idea," said Steevens, in the tone of one who keeps an open mind.
> "I believe it will smash – flat," said the lieutenant.

"He seems to have calculated it all out pretty well," said Steevens, still impartial.

"But think of the pressure," said the lieutenant. "At the surface of the water it's fourteen pounds to the inch, thirty feet down it's double that . . . let's see . . . a ton and a half to the square inch. . . ."

"Sounds a lot," said Steevens, "but it's jolly thick steel."

It is now obvious to the reader that the story is about deep-sea diving, and the conflict is already present: between man and the sea. The lieutenant shows up as being very doubtful about the whole idea; Steevens is more hopeful. We are prepared, too, for the entrance of the central character – "he" in the extract – who has invented the diving bell. All these facts have been passed on to us almost without our noticing it. Compare the dreadful result if the first paragraph started:

> A scientist had made a thick steel diving bell, with which he hoped to travel into the sea.

Although this is the vital point, the reader can be led to guess at it. It is filled in as the story proceeds. In other words, we do not have to put first things first. It is better if we do not.

MIDDLES

Always the reader must be encouraged to read on. So long as there is unsolved conflict, they will want to know "what happens next". Therefore, the central part of the story must never let them guess the ending. This "keeping them guessing" is usually called suspense. As you can see, if the plot is right, suspense will take care of itself automatically.

The most frequent difficulty in the central parts of stories is the necessity of getting the facts across to the reader. To throw item after item of information at him may seem to be telling him the story. What we must do, however, is to let the story tell itself. I think this example will make it clear:

> Rhayader was sailing down the estuary at night, and Frith was standing on the sea wall watching him. It was dark, but the sky was illuminated by stars and moon and northern lights.
> Then the snow goose suddenly rose up from behind Frith, and went over the lighthouse before flying off with Rhayader, and circling his boat. Frith could see them both for a long time.
> She was worried in case Rhayader should not come back. Then, feeling rather dejected, she went back to the lighthouse.

All the while, facts are being thrown at us, worst of all facts about the feelings and emotions of Frith. By expanding the facts into a pleasing description, and allowing us to guess at Frith's feelings by her words and actions, Paul Gallico allows the story to tell itself. The extract is from his book *The Snow Goose*:

> ... It was night now, bright with moon fragments and stars and northern glow. Frith stood on the sea wall and watched the sail gliding down the swollen estuary. Suddenly, from the darkness behind her, there came a rush of wings and something swept past her into the air. In the night light she saw the flash of white wings, black-tipped, and the thrust forward head of the snow goose.
> It rose and cruised over the lighthouse and then headed down the winding creek where Rhayader's sail was slanting in the gaining breeze and flew above him, in slow, wide circles.
> White sail and white bird were visible for a long time.

"Watch o'er him. Watch o'er him," Frith whispered. When they were both out of sight at last, she turned and walked back slowly with bent head, back to the empty lighthouse.

Let the story unfold naturally.

ENDINGS

The importance of a strong ending cannot be overstressed. A reasonable story can be made from a good ending: no one can be satisfied with an otherwise brilliant story, which has a weak ending.

There are three fundamental types of ending, and all depend on the conflict triangle.

Straight endings are those which merely take the reader to the resolving of the conflict. Throughout the story, the reader will have been wondering who will win the struggle. The ending tells them just that.

The action will have moved from a struggle shown in the opening, through the suspense of the middle, to the new situation at the end. All the questions raised have been answered: the whole affair is tidy, and complete.

In *Rebecca* by Daphne du Maurier, the main action is set in an old house: Manderley. The house becomes a place of terror, in which terrible things happen. The last paragraphs of the story are these:

> . . . The hills rose in front of us, and dipped, and rose again. It was quite dark. The stars had gone.
>
> "What time did you say it was?" I asked.
>
> "Twenty past two," he said.
>
> "It's funny," I said. "It looks almost as if the dawn was breaking over there, beyond those hills. It can't be though, it's too early."
>
> "It's the wrong direction," he said, "you're looking west."

"I know," I said. "It's funny, isn't it?"

He did not answer and I went on watching the sky. It seemed to get lighter even as I stared. Like the first streak of sunrise. Little by little, it spread across the sky.

"It's in winter you see the northern lights," he said. "That's Manderley."

I glanced at him and saw his face. I saw his eyes.

"Maxim," I said. "Maxim, what is it?"

He drove fast, much faster. We topped the hill before us and saw Lanyon lying in a hollow at our feet. There, to the left of us was the silver streak of the river, widening to the estuary at Kerrith six miles away. The road to Manderley lay ahead. There was no moon. The sky above our heads was inky black. But the sky on the horizon was not dark at all. It was shot with crimson, like a splash of blood. And the ashes blew towards us with the salt wind from the sea.

The destruction of Manderley is the final act, wiping away even the scene of the conflict. We need to know no more: there is nothing more to happen.

Even here though, in the last two hundred words, the suspense is kept up. We are not sure what is happening until the last paragraph: it is only ten words from the end that the word "ashes" makes it absolutely clear what has happened.

Obviously in a novel, there will be a much more complex plot than in a short story. Everything tends to move more slowly, too. Therefore, we must hold the deciding factor back until the last possible moment. Ideally until the last word, although this is not often practicable.

The reason is that as soon as the conflict is solved, the story loses all suspense, all interest, all point. The greatest crime in an ending is to add a few sentences after the real ending has come: but it is one of the commonest faults.

Never write on, once the conflict is decided.

As a variation, the ending and the beginning may be almost identical: the story runs in a circle.

Circular endings take the characters back where they started. Much has happened in between, but it has not changed them. We feel they will run into the same conflicts again and again. This type of ending gives a story a note of hopelessness. A typical outline might be: Two school friends arguing over how to spend the first day of the holidays. The argument gets so heated that each goes off separately. By evening they have come to their senses, and are friends once more. Ending: they start arguing over how to spend the second day of the holidays.

Twist endings are the most used for short stories, since they provide a powerful and neat finish without requiring great length.

The idea is to surprise the reader with the last sentence. This may be done in two basic ways.

By holding back vital information: when this is finally given away, the story suddenly becomes clear. Detective stories often do this. The author is almost in conflict with the reader here, as to who can solve the problem first.

A plot on these lines might be:

> Description of someone cutting up a body. General mood of horror, blood on his hands, knives and saws. Girl enters: "Pound of steak, please."

This is not an easy device to handle. Too often the reader feels cheated, or the ending does not fit absolutely exactly. The result to be aimed for, is puzzlement from the reader, who then says to himself: "I should have guessed from the start."

It is an unfair trick to suddenly turn the whole story into part of a film or play in the last line. Worse still, is to try to end with "Then I woke up." Firstly, it is not a solution of the conflict; it is just a cheap way out. Secondly, dreams are *not* like real life.

If you want to try writing about dreams, then the whole atmosphere must be that of a dream: weird, fanciful and flowing from one thing to another.

A good example of waking from a dream is from *Alice in Wonderland* by Lewis Carroll:

> "Let the jury consider their verdict," said the King, for about the twentieth time that day.
>
> "No, no!" said the Queen. "Sentence first – verdict afterwards."
>
> "Stuff and nonsense!" said Alice loudly. "The idea of having the sentence first."
>
> "Hold your tongue!" said the Queen, turning purple.
>
> "I won't!" said Alice.
>
> "Off with her head!" the Queen shouted at the top of her voice. Nobody moved.
>
> "Who cares for you?" said Alice (she had grown to her full size by this time). "You're nothing but a pack of cards!"
>
> At this, the whole pack rose up into the air, and came flying down upon her: she gave a scream, half of fright and half of anger, and tried to beat them off, and found herself lying on the bank, with her head in the lap of her sister, who was gently brushing away some dead leaves that had fluttered down from the trees upon her face. . . .

The whole situation is unreal, and there is a gradual slide from dream to reality, with the leaves giving us the link.

The better type of twist ending requires a modification to the conflict triangle. There will be *two* deciding factors, the second one cancelling out the first. Just when the reader is sure he knows what the outcome is, he is shaken by the second factor.

A typical twist ending might occur like this:

> Maintenance engineer is fired by his employer for not keeping the lift in working order. He gets so furious, that he kills his employer, and then tries to escape. Someone comes up the stairs – he will be caught. He gets into the lift and is away. Then the lift jams.

Or in diagram form:

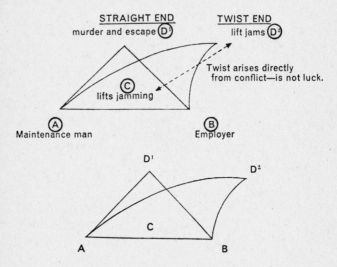

Although the twist ending is very attractive, it has one basic fault. If the reader guesses the twist in advance, then the story is wrecked. You must be careful not to give too much away, and to think out a really ingenious ending.

Twist endings must arise naturally from the story: they must not be tacked on the end. No ending must be contrived by chance, or trickery on the writer's part.

Although you may have written a story around a given title, you will usually want to find a new title that fits the story more exactly. As a general rule titles should be short – three or four words at the most – and should be your first attempt to make the reader read on.

Always leave your choice of final title to the end, because by then a phrase will usually have suggested itself. Never give too much away in the title. "*Escape from Death*" may sound well – but if the conflict in the story is between man and the risk of death, then who wants to read through it? You have wrecked it in three words! The ideal title will be interesting, because it is slightly mysterious. It will only become clear what was meant by the time the reader has finished. (This applies to short stories, where each word is so much more important. Novelists can afford to be less careful, although Michael Innes' title *Weight of the Evidence* is precisely the type in question. It provides the clue to the whole murder mystery, yet you will not realise that until the solution is expounded at the end.) Often a phrase from the last sentence will be an excellent title.

Titles must be neat and must not give the point of the story away.

Assignment 6

(a) Look back to some of your earlier stories and, with a really critical eye, see if you can cut the opening short, or end it sooner. Don't look just for sentences to cut – would it still make sense if you started reading after the second or first paragraph? Then try rewriting the opening, using the extra space you have gained by the cut, to build characters further.

(b) Do a diagram of two stories that would have twist endings, like the diagram in this section. Choose one, and write the story. Three hundred words.

(c) Write a story with an exactly circular ending, i.e. the last sentence is the same as the first. About six hundred words.

(d) Write a story with a straight ending, paying particular attention to keeping the suspense going, right from the opening.

Find *three* titles for each story you write, apart from the working title that your teacher may have offered you. Try to decide not only which is the best, but why.

7 Sentences and Paragraphs

THERE are various aspects of writing which you cannot hope to keep at the front of your mind all the while you are writing, but which are useful to examine for two reasons. First, until you see how they work in detail, you cannot expect to use them easily in your own writing. Second, when you are faced with something that you have written that you know is not a success, checking on these points may help to improve it.

The aim, however, must be to make them part of your way of writing, so that you use them automatically, without consciously thinking about it. (In much the same way as a swimmer will learn the exact positions of arms and legs for a stroke, but will not think as he swims, that he must now move his arm forward – he does it automatically.)

In this section I want to examine the various effects that can be gained by variations in the way sentences and paragraphs are built; then in the next, we can go on to look at words and word groups in more detail.

When we speak, we show where our sentences begin and end by pausing, and full-stops are often just the translation of these pauses into a visual form. But in speech we can also raise and lower our voices, give different tones to our phrases, which all help to convey the meaning exactly.

In writing, we can, by careful construction of sentences and paragraphs, lend emphasis to one part of the sentence, or convey a particular tone.

There are actually three principal ways in which sentences can be built:

A *simple* sentence makes a single statement:

(1) It was raining.

(2) The rain fell more and more heavily from the darkening sky.

Although one is much longer than the other, they both do a similar job: make one simple statement.

A *multiple* sentence is several of these simple ones joined together by "and" or "but" or "or". No one statement is given priority over the other; they are simply linked together. (If there are only two parts, it is known as a *double* sentence.)

(3) The rain fell and the sky darkened and the sun vanished behind thickening clouds.

A *complex* sentence takes two simple statements and makes one part more important than the other.

(4) As the sky darkened, the sun vanished behind thickening clouds.

(5) The sky darkened as the sun vanished behind thickening clouds.

In the first example, we lay more stress on the sun vanishing; in the second, the stress is reversed.

We can also make a mixture of the second two types. This is a *compound* sentence:

(6) While the rain fell and the sky darkened, the sun vanished behind thickening clouds.

What are the differing effects we can get by the use of these various types?

The *simple sentence* is often unjustly neglected. Obviously, if we used little else, any story would start to sound like something for children of five. When it is extended as the example (2) above, it becomes perfectly acceptable. But its most important job is in its very short, simple form when, coming after several longer sentences, it is a sudden powerful statement:

> Marius looked up at me for a moment, his head tilted back in a slight smile, as if to tell me that everything was all right. Then, very slowly, his eyelids drifted down until they completely hid his tired eyes. He was dead.

The effect of this would be lessened if the last sentence had been linked into another. It makes the one, simple, and most important statement stand out harshly and clearly.

This use of the very short sentence works best when it follows longer ones – nearly always it is at its most effective when it comes at the end of a paragraph, acting as a summary of what has gone before. Similarly, a succession of these staccato sentences can be very useful at points of climax, giving a rapid and vigorous feeling to the words:

> Ralph turned on his heel. He whipped a knife from his pocket. The cable hung above him, within easy reach. He grabbed it: cut it.

The last two sentences have run together, making them even more rapid in movement.

The *multiple sentence* has several drawbacks. It makes no one part most important, so that there is no centre of interest for the reader. We have all met (and written) the string of statements with "and" between each. This is the laziest, and worst misuse of the whole idea of linking statements.

Nevertheless, there are two ways to get maximum effect from this type of sentence. One is to leave out all the ands except the last one:

> She lifted the latch, swung the door back, stepped to one side, and motioned me to enter.

Here, we simply want to get a list of facts or actions across to the reader in the shortest possible time. No single one is of great importance. This is a useful device, so long as, like most devices, it is not over-used.

The second way is a very specialised use: it needs very careful handling, but creates a long, lazy sentence that often seems to have a ring of mystery about it:

> Then the mist drifted back and shrouded the fens from view, and the watchers turned and walked away through the damp reeds, and they did not speak; and a skein of wild geese swung overhead.

The *compound sentence* is probably the most widely used. It has the great advantage that it tends to emphasize one part of it.

The way in which a sentence is built has an effect on the tone which it conveys.

The best effect is created by using a variety of sentence styles, and varying the length, too. A short sentence has its greatest effect when it follows a long one, as we have seen. By mixing the types of sentences, and mixing long ones with short, you make the writing sound more interesting to the reader.

The actual length of a sentence is something it is obviously impossible to give much advice about. However, it is equally obvious that the longer a sentence is, the more skill it needs to write it, without it becoming confused. Despite this, the less skilled writer nearly always tries to use sentences of far too great a length. The average number of words used by various authors on a random page are:

Author	Average	Longest	Shortest
Fred Hoyle	17	42	2
Nevil Shute	14	28	5
George Orwell	18	53	4
John Buchan	20	38	6
2nd Former	21	30	14

I am *not* suggesting that you should solemnly count the words you use in each sentence. I *am* suggesting that you should beware of too many long sentences, and of lack of variation in sentence length.

Something of the same warning holds good for paragraphs. The function of a paragraph is to divide up your writing into easily digestible mouthfuls for your reader. The sheer indigestible nature of a solid page of writing, with not a division in sight, tends to make anyone shy away from reading. Therefore, keep paragraphs fairly short – vary them in length – set them well in from the margin – and the page looks inviting.

Within reason, therefore, you should be out to help your reader by dividing the writing into small, simple units, making it as easy to understand as possible. Any excuse for a change of paragraph is worth considering.

You *must* change paragraphs whenever you begin to write about a different person, if they are speaking. The paragraph division does not come when they start to speak – it comes when they become the subject of the paragraphs:

> "Will you do it?" I asked.
> Bill shook his head.
> "Think again," I urged.

The centre paragraph concerns Bill. He has the whole paragraph to himself.

You can also change paragraphs when there is a change of time, or of scene, or of mood.

As a general rule, the first and last paragraphs of a story should be kept as short as possible. It gives a rapid start, and a neat ending. Even a single sentence can stand alone as a paragraph.

The general rule to bear in mind, is that sentences and paragraphs are only devices to help the reader to follow what you mean as easily as possible. If your reader does not understand, then you are failing in your writing, just as much as an actor fails if he cannot be heard.

Just what a difference good paragraphing and sentence building can make is shown by the two passages below. In the first, I have deliberately destroyed the real arrangement, running sentences and paragraphs together:

> Then something awoke me. The old man laid down his hand to light a cigar but he didn't pick it up at once, but sat back for a moment in his chair, with his fingers tapping his knees, which was the movement I remem-

bered when I had stood before him in the moorland farm with the pistols of his servants behind me. A little thing, lasting only a second, and the odds were a thousand to one that I might have had my eyes on my cards at the time and missed it, but I didn't. In a flash the air seemed to clear, and some shadow lifted from my brain.

I was looking at the three men with full and absolute recognition as the clock on the mantelpiece struck ten o'clock, when the three faces seemed to change before my eyes and reveal their secrets.

The young one was the murderer because now I saw cruelty and ruthlessness, where before I had only seen good humour. His knife, I made certain, had skewered Skudder to the floor, and his kind had put the bullet in Karolides.

The plump man's features seemed to dislimn, and form again, as I looked at them. He hadn't a face. He had only a hundred masks which he could assume again when he pleased so that chap must have been a superb actor.

Now here is the original from *The Thirty-Nine Steps* by John Buchan. The sentences are shorter, and so are the paragraphs. Each point is made to stand out with far more force. The words are virtually the same: it is the arrangement of them by means of punctuation which makes such an extraordinary difference:

Then something awoke me.

The old man laid down his hand to light his cigar. He didn't pick it up at once, but sat back for a moment in his chair, with his fingers tapping his knees.

It was the movement I remembered when I had stood before him in the moorland farm, with the pistols of his servants behind me.

A little thing, lasting only a second, and the odds were a thousand to one that I might have had my eyes on my cards at the time and missed it. But I didn't, and, in a flash, the air seemed clear. Some shadow lifted from my brain, and I was looking at the three men with full and absolute recognition.

The clock on the mantelpiece struck ten o'clock.

The three faces seemed to change before my eyes and reveal their secrets. The young one was the murderer. Now I saw the cruelty and ruthlessness, where before I had only seen good humour. His knife, I made certain, had skewered Skudder to the floor. His kind had put the bullet in Karolides.

The plump man's features seemed to dislimn, and form again, as I looked at them. He hadn't a face, only a hundred masks that he could assume when he pleased. That chap must have been a superb actor. . . .

There is nothing grammatically wrong with the first version, but it is bad none the less. Punctuation is more than a matter of being correct; it should be *used* to make each point cry out for the reader's attention.

Good paragraph and sentence construction can add to the effectiveness of the story.

Assignment 7

Although much of this assignment may seem rather odd, if you appreciate that you, the writer, must always be in control of the words, I think you will see the point of it. No one in their right mind is going to write a story by planning how many words go in each sentence: but they should have the skill to do so, if asked. Once you get pushed around by words, and cannot control sentences properly, then you are losing your grip. You must be the master of the words, not the other way round.

(a) Write a passage of four simple sentences.

(b) And one with four multiple sentences.

(c) Write a third one with four compound sentences.

(d) Taking either *The Boat* or *A Car* or *Seashore* as your subject, write a passage that fits the length plan shown below. Each line is a paragraph; each number the number of words in each sentence. You should find you are using various types of sentence, because the plan rather invites it.

Plan:

      4.
      8 . . . 17 . . . 10 . . . 6.
      22.
      25 . . . 13 . . . 7.

8 Words

ONE of the more fortunate things about English as a language is that it has an enormous vocabulary. This is because, although we think of it as one language, it is, in fact, the result of a mixture of languages.

Often we have several words with much the same meaning, borrowed at different times from different languages. Town, village and city all mean a collection of dwellings; the first is Anglo-Saxon, the second French, the last Latin. They all now have distinct meanings.

Sometimes the distinction is not in meaning, but in attitude. To refer to a girl as slim, is polite. Thin, not so polite. Skinny, is plain rude. The girl has not changed in shape, but the *overtones* of the word are different.

Hovel, hut, dwelling, house, hall, mansion, palace: each has a tone. Hovel is ugly; hut, primitive, but not necessarily unpleasant; dwelling is vague; house is normal enough, too; a hall is rather grand, and a mansion better. A palace is the most luxurious.

Words carry more than just meaning: they have important overtones.

"The golden orb swept above the mountain crests"

is rather grand. "The sun popped up from behind the top of the hills" is much less imposing. Yet both describe the same scene.

The best way of appreciating how wide a choice of words you have, is to look at Roget's *Thesaurus*. Here, words with similar meanings are collected. For example, looking for a word to describe an iceberg, we can refer to "cold" in the index, are sent to section 383 and given this list:

> cold, cool, chill, chilly, gelid, frigid, algid, fresh, keen, bleak, raw, inclement, bitter, biting, niveous, cutting, nipping, piercing, pinching, clay-cold, icy, glacial, frosty, freezing, wintry, brumal, hibernal, boreal, arctic, Siberian. . . .

As a way of improving your vocabulary, it is excellent. As an aid to memory, when the exact word you want escapes you, it is good, too. But beware of picking words that you are unfamiliar with – they may have the wrong overtones. There would be something odd about describing an antarctic iceberg as Siberian.

The result of this rich vocabulary and wide usage has been that the more fanciful and imaginative uses of language have flourished in English much more than in other, more limited and workmanlike languages, where it is only possible to say one thing in one way. More often though, we create effects not with single words, but with groups of them. These devices are called "figurative" to distinguish them from the normal "literal" ways of expressing ideas.

Literal usage means saying exactly what we mean:
The traitor has been killed. (a)
The clouds were white. (b)

81

Figurative language does not say exactly what is meant. It expresses its idea by means of a picture, often saying something that is not completely true, but which can be readily understood.

The traitor has been liquidated. (a)

The clouds were like ivory. (b)

The first pair of statements are simple. The second two are more expressive, more forceful. (a) Gives the impression that the man has been destroyed without trace. What it actually says, though, is that he has been turned into liquid – which is not *literally* so. (Unless perhaps he had been boiled in oil.) (b) Does not mean the clouds were hard as ivory is: the comparison is only between the creamy-whiteness of ivory and the colour of the cloud.

Figurative language is more powerful and interesting.

There are three main classes of figurative language that we can examine in detail. They have rather clumsy names, but the names are useful in that they describe what actually happens in the device.

"*Simile*" is Latin for "like" and we frequently say one thing is like another, without meaning it literally.

e.g. She eats like a pig.

Translated into literal terms, we mean: "She is extremely greedy, and has bad table manners" or something of the sort. We do not mean that she eats out of a trough, on all fours in a farmyard.

"*Metaphor*" is Greek, for "change of sense". While a simile states one thing is like another, the metaphor goes the whole way and states it actually *is* something else.

e.g. She is a pig when she is eating.

"Personification" means "making into a person". This is a less used figure of speech, but with care, can be effective.

e.g. The town-hall clock stared down on empty streets.

The word "stare" really means doing something which only a person can do. The clock has been made into a person to render the sentence more vivid.

The real point at issue is how useful these devices are to us in making writing more effective – and the answer, as usual, is a double one. Figurative language can indeed make writing more interesting to the reader, if it is well done. If it is done badly, then it is a positive handicap, making the writing dull and dead.

The trouble is, that a really interesting idea, once it has been used often, becomes so familiar and ordinary, that it no longer carries any impact at all. A dead figurative use is called a *"Cliché"*.

> When he had *told his boss what he thought of him*, he realised that he had *burnt his boats*, so he *threw up* his job. Then he *brought to mind*, that *many moons ago*, the head of a rival firm had *set great store* by his advice. He *dropped a line* to the firm, and until the reply came, was *like a cat on hot bricks*.

This is a terrible second-hand piece of writing: nearly half of it is composed of phrases and ideas that are borrowed complete from other people's writing.

"Burning one's boats" was once a very lively phrase – referring to Julius Caesar who did just this, to stop his army from thinking that they could retreat in safety.

"Like a cat on hot bricks" is a wonderful way of describing someone who is agitated and cannot keep still – or it *was* a wonderful way, until it became so common that it lost its impact.

Although I said earlier that it was possible to borrow ideas, remember that they must not be borrowed in lumps like this. "As cold as ice" and "as warm as toast" are clichés, and should be avoided: "As chilly as ice-cream" and "as hot as buttered crumpets" are not. They are perfectly usable phrases, but you can see clearly enough that I have borrowed the ideas.

This is not to say that we must for ever be forcing striking and original phrases on the reader's attention: this could be distracting to him. He would begin to study the phrases and forget the main story you were trying to tell.

Scattered here and there, they add an extra sparkle to a passage while the cliché only adds tarnish.

Figurative language is lively if it is fresh: dead if it is stale and full of clichés.

Oscar Wilde has a happy knack of using words in just such a lively way. Often, he draws our attention to a word by giving it an unusual sense, and making us think more deeply about the word itself, and about what he means:

> . . . The sullen murmur of the bees shouldering their way through the long unmown grass, or circling with monotonous insistence round the dusty gilt horns of the straggling woodbine, seemed to make the stillness more oppressive. The dim roar of London was like the bourdon note of a distant organ.
>
> *The Picture of Dorian Gray.*

The bees "shouldering" their way around, making us feel they are loaded down with honey, and the comparison of London traffic in the distance with the

84

deep bass note of an organ, really bring the scene to life. There are various other words, though, that are not literal: "sullen", "dusty", "horns", "dim".

The question of how to find these telling phrases is one that you have to answer for yourself; originality is all important. So long as you are aware of similes, metaphors and personification – whether you remember the names or not – the chances are that ideas for lively words will start to come.

One way of starting to develop this side of your writing is by looking for "doublets" (there is no official name for these, so I have had to invent one).

Doublets are made by taking one word – usually a noun – that you were going to use anyway, and deliberately looking for an unlikely one to go with it. The first consideration is that it must make real sense, of course – it must do a real job of work; but the second is that it should be really unusual and alive. Sometimes you can actually invent a new word by coupling two together with a hyphen.

> e.g. Umbrella April; icicle December; wind-whispering grass; skin-popping sausages.

Dylan Thomas was adept at this type of word-spinning:

> . . . It is night in the chill, squat chapel, hymning in bonnet and brooch and bombazine black, butterfly choker and bootlace bow coughing like nannygoats, sucking mintoes, fortywinking hallelujahs; night in the four-ale, quiet as domino; in Ocky Milkman's lofts like a mouse with gloves; in Dai Bread's bakery flying like black flour. It is tonight in Donkey Street, trotting silent, with seaweed on its hooves, along cockled streets, past curtained fernpot, text and trinket, harmonium, holy

dresser, watercolours done by hand, china dog and rosy
tin teacaddy. It is night eddying among the snuggeries
of babies.

Under Milk Wood.

In this picture of a Welsh village at night, we can
see how he picks out definite nouns to paint in the
details of the scene. More than this though, we are
given striking similes like "coughing like nannygoats"
and doublets like "fortywinking hallelujahs". The
whole passage races on with not a dull word in sight:
no clichés here.

People are sometimes puzzled by the idea of *repetition*. To use the same word twice in close proximity,
is a mistake if it is just the result of lack of care in
choice of words. The result is clumsy:

> e.g. The antique-dealer's window was filled with a
> wonderful collection of rusting and dusty swords, dag-
> gers, and antique pistols.

Intentionally used, however, repetition has a pleasing ring. Just to make certain it is not taken for a mistake, I think that it is best to use the word three times,
rather than just twice.

> e.g. The gold of the sun swept down through the gold
> of the clouds and left nothing alight but a fading gold
> path on the sea.

Similarly, the pattern of one half can be repeated in
the second half:

> e.g. The damp of the cobbled pathway rose and chilled
> my feet: the damp of the driving rain fell and chilled my
> face.

*The first function of words is to convey meaning: if
we can add to the meaning by creating striking phrases*

and more exciting ways of expression, then this adds to the effect on the reader.

Assignment 8

Although you are being asked to try out some of these devices as separate items, do not lose sight of the real point – that they must be brought into your writing naturally and usefully. There is no merit in decoration for your own amusement.

(a 1) Complete the following phrases, *not* with the normal words. You do not deserve a mark if anyone else in the form has the same answer:

As cold as ....
As black as ....
As lively as ....
As dead as ....
As fat as ....
As innocent as ....
As wet as ....
As pale as ....
As true as ....
As wild as ....

(a 2) Make some unusual doublets for the months of the year, e.g. Snowman January.

(b) Construct a paragraph of about seventy-five words using at least five metaphors. Underline them.

(c) Write down five clichés, and then re-write them, trying to bring them to life again.

(d) Introduce some repetition into a sentence, and try to describe the extra effect it has given it.

(e) Read the Dylan Thomas passage again, and try a description of your own town in a similar way (about one hundred words).

9 Style

> . . . Then she let them down by a cord through the
> window: for her house was upon the town wall, and she
> dwelt upon the wall. And she said unto them, Get you to
> the mountain, lest the pursuers meet you; and hide your-
> selves there three days, until the pursuers be returned:
> and afterwards may ye go your way. And the men said
> unto her: We will be blameless of this thine oath which
> thou has made us swear . . .

I THINK you will have been fairly certain that this
passage came from the Bible, even though it is unlikely that you remember reading it, and it is probable
that you have never read it. Nevertheless, the whole
style of it says "Bible" quite clearly.

If you have a really wide knowledge of literature, you will be able to recognise authors, and periods
of literature, even though you have never read the
actual pieces in question.

What is it that enables us to make these judge-
ments? Sometimes the subject matter helps, though I
chose a passage that did not mention any obvious
Bible names or subjects. Usually it is the sum of
many small points that help us to these conclusions.
Vocabulary ("ye" and "thine" are not used in modern

writing; "dwelt" is going out of use too, and "cord" is used where we would say "rope"); sentence construction (the long flowing sentences using "and" and "for" as joining words); the repetition of an idea (house on the wall, dwelt on the wall) – all these small points go to make up the general notion of *style*.

Style is the overall result of the various devices a writer uses.

At first, you may think that you have not a real style of your own – and you will be right. Each time you are introduced to a new idea in writing, as you will have been while you have worked through this book, it will probably make a slight change in your style.

Each time you read a book, you will be affected by the ideas and writing methods in it. Again, it looks at first sight as if all style is second-hand; merely borrowings from other people. To some extent this is true, but it is a misleading way of looking at the problem. Just how much, and of what element you borrow is your own decision – probably made unconsciously.

For the moment, the great thing is to avoid picking up points of style that can be called bad, and therefore I want to look at some of the commonest bad writing habits.

A definition of bad style is simple: *Bad style means using words in an inefficient way*.

If we say that a tennis-player has a bad style, we mean that even though he may be reasonably successful, he plays in such a way that he will never be able to improve beyond a certain stage. He is playing in an inefficient way.

We have already looked at the cliché – this is a

good example of a fault in style. The words are no longer doing all the work they should.

There will always be some people who will not like some perfectly efficient ways of writing: but this is a matter of taste. Just because you do not like the way someone writes does not mean his style is bad. If you can prove that he can say what he wants to more clearly, more powerfully, or with fewer words, then you are perfectly entitled to call that style bad.

Style is nothing to do with decoration: it is to do with getting the ideas over to the reader in the best possible way.

This does not mean that there is only one best way – there are hundreds. If you look back through your exercise book, you will probably find that your handwriting has changed over the past year. It will go on changing for some time, until eventually it will be so characteristic of you, that it will be as personal as a fingerprint. Your writing style will do the same thing. Just as bad handwriting is difficult to read – and therefore inefficient – so bad style is inefficient. But there are as many good styles of handwriting as there are legible writers.

As soon as writers start experimenting with words, enlarging their vocabulary, getting the feel of complicated sentences, they nearly always fall into the trap of thinking that complexity is a virtue. They write this sort of sentence:

> John suffered the affliction of the common cold during a period of nearly two weeks. The local practitioner provided him with a selection of medicaments for the ailment.

They feel that such writing shows just how well

they can handle words; that they have a good command of vocabulary; and are very hurt to be told that this is bad style.

Nevertheless, if we try the final test on it, we find that the real sense is:

> John had a cold for a fortnight, and the doctor gave him some medicine.

But the first example uses twenty-nine words, and the second fourteen to convey exactly the same sense. We have increased the efficiency of the writing by over one hundred per cent.

This does not mean that long words are not useful: often they have very precise meanings that would take several simpler words to convey. Long words can be a help to brevity:

> The doctor put a thing for seeing how hot he was in his mouth.

is far better phrased:

> The doctor put a thermometer in his mouth.

or better still:

> The doctor took his temperature.

Never use two words where one will do. Never use a long word where a short one will do.

There are plenty of other styles to avoid. The worst ones are the artificial ones: the newspaper gossip-columnist who tries to make interesting reading from what the film star had for breakfast; the sports writer who always describes a football match as extremely good, or extremely bad; the record critic who uses his own peculiar language to describe the latest popular song.

All these have one thing in common: they are trying to make rather dull material into something more. It is an impossible task. The cheaper newspapers that manage to find a sensational piece of news, even when nothing of importance has happened, use the same overdone style. The writing has become decorative again.

This over-writing – deliberate sensationalism – has no place in a short story. If the plot is interesting, there is no need to do it. If it is not, then scrap it and start again.

That does not mean that all newspaper writing is bad: for clear, factual, informative writing the responsible papers are well worth studying.

They say what they want to, without frills.

Style is not a decoration to be added to writing. It is merely a tool for the most effective expression of ideas.

Therefore it follows that your own style will arise naturally from within your work. Although it would be a mistake to deliberately copy a style – apart from the odd exercise – your own style will depend very much on what you read. Reading authors with a good style (by which I do not mean only the "classics", but the sort of books suggested in the reading list) will help you to develop a good style of your own.

The three extracts which follow all have a characteristic flavour about them. Even so, they all are clear and straightforward. They are not quoted as being masterpieces of literature, but of good, sensible ways of writing:

Dodie Smith at the opening of *I Capture the Castle* wants us to get to know the main character quickly, and the surroundings in which she lives. It is an easy, chatty style concerned with the thoughts of the character. Even though there is no direct speech, we feel she is talking directly to us – with a delightful mixture of girlish romance and hard common sense. Very simple, very conversational – but the points made to the reader are clear. We forget we are reading, and start to be in the castle in our imagination. Therefore the writing is a success:

> . . . I write this sitting in the kitchen sink. That is, my feet are in it; the rest of me is on the draining board, which I have padded with our dog's blanket and the tea-cosy. I can't say that I am really comfortable, and there is a depressing smell of carbolic soap, but this is the only part of the kitchen where there is any daylight left. And I have found that sitting in a place where you have never sat before can be inspiring – I wrote my best poem while sitting on the hen-house. Though even that isn't a very good poem. I have decided that my poetry is so bad that I mustn't write any more of it.
>
> Drips from the walls are plopping into the water-butt by the back door. The view from the window is excessively drear. Beyond the dank garden in the courtyard are the ruined walls on the edge of the moat. Beyond the moat, the boggy, ploughed fields stretch to the leaden sky. I tell myself that all the rain we have had is good for nature, and that at any moment spring will surge on us. I try to see leaves on the trees and the courtyard filled with sunlight. Unfortunately, the more my mind's eye sees green and gold, the more drained of all its colour the twilight seems.
>
> It is comforting to look away from the windows and towards the kitchen fire, near which my sister Rose is ironing – though she obviously can't see properly, and it will be a pity if she scorches her only nightgown. (I have two, but one is minus its behind.) Rose looks particularly fetching by firelight because she is a pinkish person: her skin has a pink glow and her hair is pinkish gold, very light and feathery. Although I am rather used to her

I know she is a beauty. She is nearly twenty-one and very bitter with life. I am seventeen, look younger, feel older. I am no beauty, but have a neatish face.

I have just remarked to Rose that our situation is rather romantic – two girls in this strange and lonely house. She replied that she saw nothing romantic about being shut up in a crumbling ruin surrounded by a sea of mud. I must admit that our home is an unreasonable place to live in. Yet I love it.

Nevil Shute was an aircraft designer, and in *No Highway* he used his technical knowledge to paint a convincing background for us. All the same, it is never so technical that we do not understand it. The long description with which the passage ends holds our attention easily – simply because there is a conflict, and we must know what the result will be. The style is hardly noticeable: it just gets on with the job of telling us what happened, in a good, strong, straightforward manner:

(Mr. Honey is an aeronautical scientist who believes that the aircraft on which he is travelling may crash because of metal fatigue. But he has no real evidence to support him and the pilot and the air safety officer decide to fly on.)

. . . Mr. Honey, nearly in tears with weariness and frustration, said "I assure you . . . I assure you that's the wrong thing to do. It's absolutely courting disaster to go on. You *must* ground this aircraft. Really you must."

Samuleson glanced at Symes, and their eyes met in complete agreement; this was not a normal, reasonable man. This was an eccentric, plugging away at a fixed idea, a man whose mental balance was abnormal.

"If you would rather stay here, Mr. Honey," the captain said, "I can make arrangements for you to finish the journey in another craft, probably tomorrow. But I'm afraid I can't listen to any more of this."

The inspector nodded in agreement. This Reindeer would be off before long, and he could get to bed and have a couple of hours more before breakfast. Then, in the course of the morning, he would write out a report on the incident and send it in to his own headquarters. Two copies would be sufficient, and one for his own file.

Honey said desperately, "Is that your final decision? You're really going on?"

"I assure you . . ." Mr. Honey's voice died in despair; it was useless to go on trying to convince these men. He turned forward to the pilots' seats, and then, quite nonchalantly, he put his hand upon the undercarriage operating lever and pulled it to "Up".

He did so so quietly that it did not register with anybody for an instant; Symes was the only man present who actually saw him do it, and it took a second or two for the inspector to appreciate what was happening. Then he cried, "Here – stop that!"

The note of the auxiliary motor changed as the load came on the dynamo. Samuleson turned, saw what Honey was doing, and made a dive for the lever.

Mr. Honey flung his body up against the pedestal, covering the controls. He said, half weeping, "If you won't ground this aircraft, I will."

The motors of the retracting mechanism groaned, the solid floor beneath their feet sagging ominously. Cousins, with quick wit, leaped for the electrical control panel and threw out the main switch to cut the current from all circuits. He was a fraction of a second too late. The undercarriage of the Reindeer was just over the dead centre. She paused for a moment; for an instant Samuleson thought Cousins had saved her, as he struggled to pull Honey from the pedestal. Then she sagged forward, and the undercarriage folded up with a sharp whistling noise from the hydraulics. A pipe burst and fluid sprayed the ground beneath her, and she sank down on her belly on the concrete apron, all the seventy-two tons of her. By the mercy of providence, nobody was standing underneath her at the time.

The noise of the crumpling panels and propellers, a

tinny metallic, crunching noise, brought the mechanics running to the wide doors of the hangars.

Marjorie Corder, going from the Reindeer to the reception and booking hall, turned at the mouth of the passage and stared aghast to see her Reindeer lying wrecked upon the tarmac. Instinctively, she began to run back towards it, horrified; she met Dobson running back from the machine to the control.

She cried, "What happened?"

He paused for an instant. "The boffin did it," he said furiously. "I told you that he'd put the kiss of death on it. Well, now he has!" . . .

The last piece is from *A Bullet in the Ballet* by Caryl Brahms and S. J. Simon. Here the style is very obvious, mainly because it is all part of the fun. The subject is very artistic and serious. The style is anything but that. It is deliberately using very ordinary words where you expect something more exotic, and treats the serious ballet of *Swan Lake* with anything but reverence. It is this odd mixture that creates the humour:

(A murder has been committed in the ballet company run by M. Stroganoff. The detective therefore needs to understand the precise arrangement of the performance – and so do the readers. The factual information has to be made palatable.)

. . . As to the presentation of *Lac des Cygnes* there are two schools of thought. School One presents the ballet in four irrelevant acts. In addition, it supplies a fleet of cardboard ducks and trails them triumphantly across the painted waters of the backcloth to well-timed gasps of admiration. School Two abolishes the birds and admiration, and stops short only of abolishing the entire ballet, condensing it into a single act, which sends the unseasoned ballet-goer away with the unfortunate impression that the hero has been left alive after all.

Stroganoff, with great resource, combined both methods. He gave the ballet in one act, but inserted all the more formidable features of the other three. He reduced the pictured lake to the dimensions of a puddle, but rolled on a couple of tipsy-looking turkeys. Puthyk proudly collected these masterpieces of carpentry as they arrived in the wings, and trundled them round the back, ready for despatch upon another voyage at the end of the ballet.

Tonight the birds were tired and stopped halfway across.

Assignment 9

(a) Continue any of the three main extracts, trying to make your own style fit with that of the extract. If you can do that, then you have a good understanding of how that style works. (About three hundred words.)

(b) Have a look at one of your earlier assignments. How would you describe your own style? What faults can you find in it? Does it seem to have changed since the beginning of term and if so, how? Write your answers down in about one hundred words.

(c) Find an example of what you consider bad style, probably from one of the sources noted in the chapter. In fifty words say what you think is wrong with it.

(d) Read the extracts again, and see how the characterisation and backgrounds are handled. Explain what devices the writers are using, again in about fifty words *each*.

(e) Try a complete six hundred word story, and bear in mind clarity of expression all the time.

(f) Talking point: re-read the preface, and discuss whether an author's style is a product of his skill, his art, or both.

10 Insulting the Reader

WHATEVER you are writing, you must bear in mind the person you expect to read it.

It is not just clumsy style, but insulting to your reader if you tell of climbing the Eiffel Tower, and then carefully inform him that it is in Paris. He knows – or even if he does not, then give him the benefit of the doubt.

Telling the reader the obvious will always make him dislike you and therefore your writing. Always try to tell the reader just sufficient for him to understand. That way, he will have to think as he reads, and will enjoy it more. If the murderer has been tracked down and caught by the police, he does not want to know that he was eventually tried and sentenced. Of course he was. If someone has just broken into tears and threatened suicide, it is not the place to explain to the reader that she is upset.

(Just in case you have found that somewhere in this book I have broken this rule, let me explain that: (a) this is not fiction, but fact, where every point *must* be made crystal clear, and (b) that it may be read by someone younger than you.)

Other ways of insulting the reader are by bad layout. The reader should not have to strain to read bad writing. Nor should he have to sort out a tangle of nonsense caused by bad punctuation. Nor should he have to work out what a word should have been because of incorrect spelling. It is irritating, and time-wasting.

More important, if he has to do this, any drama and excitement you have created will be spoilt. Your story will have less power because of its clumsy presentation.

My handwriting, I confess, is dreadful, so I use a typewriter. All I can suggest is that when you make your final copy, you make sure it is readable. It does not have to be a work of art – just absolutely clear.

There is no excuse for incorrect spelling – you can always consult a dictionary if in doubt; usually though, the mistakes creep in through carelessness. Much the same applies to punctuation. Anyone can make a slip as they are rushing to get a story down while it is clear in their minds. What is inexcusable, if you really care about your writing at all, is to present your reader with an unchecked, careless mess. You would not expect a book from the library to be illegible, with mistakes on every page; and I think the standard of a book is the one to aim at.

I am not trying to say that good writers are good spellers. Often they are not. It is far more important and skilful to be able to thread words into an interesting pattern. But if you can learn to do this, and have real pride in your work, then it is a pity to spoil the final effect for want of a little care.

Assignment 10
Complete freedom this time: go ahead and write –

just what you like, as long as you like, so long as you enjoy it. But be polite to your readers. If you are stuck for a subject, here are some ideas. Pick one point from each column: this gives you three thousand possible stories:

Reasons for Conflict	Main Character	Person	Setting	Ending
Greed	Schoolgirl	1st	Church	Straight
Pride	Mother	3rd	Pub	Twist
Jealousy	Sculptor		India	Circular
Murder	Mechanic		Shop	
Love	Actor		Street	
Power	Politician		Kitchen	
Misunderstanding	Teacher		Building-site	
	Pianist			
	Forester		Coffee Bar	
	Whaler		Night Club	
			Aircraft	

Check List

HERE is a brief outline of the points we have covered in the book. If you check through these after you have written a story, and feel that it stands up to these tests, then you can feel that you are well on the way to writing a good story. The final test though, will always be how much your readers like it:

1. Is there real conflict in the story? Is there too much happening? Check that the deciding factor is not chance.

2. Do the backgrounds make you feel you are really there? Check that they contain some fine detail and are not "out-of-focus" because of vague statements. Does it hold up the story?

3. Have you kept the number of characters to a minimum? Have they really come alive, or are they just puppets?

4. Have you included some conversation? Does it demonstrate the characters of the story? Does the story stop while you do some characterisation?

5. Is there anything which a reader is likely to reject as impossible?

6. Can you cut the opening sentence or paragraph

without losing anything? If so, do so. Can you cut the last sentence or paragraph without losing anything? If so, do so.

7. Are the paragraphs and sentences fairly short? Would it be easier for the reader to follow, if they were split up more? Is there enough variety in length and type of construction? Does it sound pleasant if read aloud?

8. Have you used any clichés? Are there any points where the language needs enlivening by figurative usage? Refer to Roget's *Thesaurus* if necessary.

9. Could any sentences be shortened without losing their sense? Are there any clumsy phrases which could be put in one word? Are there any long words which could be replaced, without loss, by shorter ones?

10. Check spelling and punctuation – refer to a dictionary if necessary.

When you can bear these points in mind as you write, then you have no further need of this book. Get rid of it. You are on your own. What you can never discard is the informed critic.

Illustrative Material

THE stories which follow have all been written by one of my pupils, a fifteen-year-old girl, in her fifth-form year. Until starting on the course, she had done little in the way of writing. Having learnt the technical side, however, she applied it, contributed her own ideas and personal approach. This is the combination of skill and art mentioned before.

There are some comments on each of these stories on pages 114 to 120, but it is better if you analyse them yourself, using the check list at the end of Chapter 10.

See if you can discover any weaknesses – and how she has covered her strong points. Consider her choice of subjects and how she has mixed situations she might have actually experienced with imaginary ones. You might also decide how you would have handled some of the topics yourself: a different approach or a change in characterisation. Notice especially her endings. She has made each one a forceful part of her story, whatever type she has chosen to adopt, and the reader is never left with a sense of inadequacy.

POLAR BEARS

When I was a toddler, there stood, above the fire-place of my nursery, three tiny wooden bears. I had never seen a polar bear, but I had heard about them in stories. These little fellows were exactly as I imagined polar bears to be. They were deep chocolate brown, half-an-inch long, and they were smiling. That was what pleased me about them: I hated anything cross or angry, and a bear that smiled suited my taste exactly.

We played endless games together, my bears and I. They were cold, so I lent them my new coat; they were hungry, so I fed them on peaches and chips. This Good Samaritan act worked the other way round. I was tired, so they carried me; I was lost, so they found me; and so it went on.

In my imagination they were any size from that of a fly to as big as I was. They were never, ever, bigger than I was.

When my birthday came, I was given a pair of bunny-wool slippers, a kitten, and, best of all, a trip to the zoo as a special treat.

We set out after dinner. There had been a few tears because I had wanted to wear my bunny-wool slippers, but I had eventually been persuaded that they would spoil in the rain.

When we reached the zoo, I was skipping with excitement. I was allowed to choose where I wanted to go, so we set off towards the bear house. Entering, I looked at the huge, dirty-grey creatures growling and scratching in the pit below. How glad I was that my bears were not like that!

My mother laughed and said: "Look at the polar bears, darling!"

I screamed and kicked and spat.

When we got home I threw the little wooden bears on the fire. I will never forgive them for the first disillusion I ever had.

GRANDPA

The organ played sweet, solemn music. Aunt Beatrice and Aunt Victoria muffled their sobs and together we shuffled slowly out of the church. Grandad lay pink, quiet and dead. It was probably the only time he had ever been quiet, and certainly the only time he had ever been dead.

Then we crowded into Gran's little house to hear the Will read.

We were all worried about the Will. We kept thinking about the times he put crushed Oxo in the coffee tin. He'd thought *that* was funny! What if he had decided it would be funny to leave his money to the Darts' Club at the *Hare 'n' Hounds*?

The lawyer came in, and the air was tense with crossed fingers and gritted teeth. No, it was all right. He'd left his money to Gran, his property to Jack and me, and the recipe for his famous cider had been left to Cousin Wilfred.

I must admit we were a bit surprised at Wilfred getting anything. Grandpa had never liked him, and had even refused to go to his wedding. I can't really blame Grandad, because Wilfred had a face that you wouldn't mind seeing on a toad, and to go with this amphibious countenance, he had greenish-black hair, parted in the middle. But apart from these faults, he was quite a nice fellow.

We thought Wilfred would sell the recipe, but he

decided to keep it and make the cider for his own private use.

When Wilfred brought the recipe to our house along with the ingredients, I was somewhat anxious, because the things he had brought were so queer.

I asked Wilfred if he'd ever made it before. He said: "No, but it's fairly easy. All the directions are written out clearly."

So there was nothing I could do but let him go ahead with it.

When the cider was finished, it did bear a vague resemblance to cider, only it looked a bit greenish. Wilfred drank some; then he also went a bit greenish.

The organ played sweet, solemn music. Aunt Beatrice and Aunt Victoria muffled their sobs. . . .

BLUE ENDING

She ran from the house into the streets. And on. And on.

A small figure in a blue coat: blending with the dusky blue of the sky, and the inky blue of rain-drenched streets, lit by the silvery-blue of street lamps.

The murmur of voices pricked the air – meaningless, empty chatter; talk for its own sake. They were all women with blue-yellow hair and blue-red lips. Lonely women: always together, always talking, always lonely. Never loving, never hating, never living; just existing.

Running over the bridge she paused to think. She had never loved; but she had hated. She still did.

She hated her brother and his wife. They'd never let her alone. Always saying she looked lonely. "A poor little lonely orphan." That's what they *wanted* her to be. But she wasn't and she wouldn't be. Couldn't they understand? She wasn't lonely: she just liked to be alone.

She had never really lived. She had tried to, but they wouldn't let her. They wouldn't let her just be by herself and simply live. Instead, they tried to goad her into only existing – doing what everyone else did, being one of the crowd, one of that vast, blank, muttering crowd. She wouldn't be! She'd sooner die!

The cool blue water caught her in a sapphire embrace. Stroking her; soothing her. She wanted to live not exist. . . .

Stroking her; soothing her. . . .

She wanted not to be lonely. . . .

She did not exist.

ANTIQUE ROSES

"Good-bye, darling – be good!"

I nodded, smiled, and took no notice of the end bit of her sentence as my mother waved goodbye to me, alternating her goodbyes with warnings about the evil ways of life in the big city. I was going to London for two whole weeks, and had no intentions of wasting them by being good.

The train drew slowly away from the platform, and, at last, Mother was just a tiny speck. I felt a thrill of excitement. I was alone. I beamed happily, if a little idiotically, out of the train window. We were passing by the old medieval castle, and the morning sun shone on the tall head-dresses of the ladies walking in the gardens.

They were pretty, gauzy little creatures in pinks,

blues and lemons; their long dresses fell in graceful folds to the ground. Their head-dresses had wisps of muslin floating from them, and this gave them an unnatural appearance, almost as though they had long been dead.

The train passed on, leaving the castle grey and misty behind me. We were passing a group of people watching a masquerade. The contrast between the black and white house with its gay inhabitants, and the pale, misty castle was quaint. How strange that neighbours can be so different!

The people were dressed in deep rich damasks and silks of purple, gold, red and sapphire blue – all deep rich colours. Skirts were full, and stiff collars sparkled white in the sun. Hair and hats alike, were studded with jewels and feathers. Everything was bright and glittering. The train moved on, racing relentlessly ahead.

We pulled in at a station; the people crowded on the platform, laughing, and welcoming home relations and friends, most of whom were soldiers in their red uniforms. Some were wounded, and judging from some of the women's faces, some were simply not there. Little girls in poke bonnets, miniature crinolines and white pantalettes, clung to precious fathers. Women in their holiday clothes cried over dear husbands. A little girl in her best blue silk, but with her face wet with tears, came up to the window. She handed me a little nosegay of pink roses.

I thought she had mistaken me for someone she knew, and was about to say so, when she said, "My daddy hasn't come home."

I understood why she couldn't take the roses home, and smiled encouragingly at her, and she joined her quiet, dignified little mother – a quiet, dignified little widow.

The train drew in at Paddington with a jerk. I opened my eyes thinking how life-like dreams were, and snatching up my suitcase, I ran to meet my laughing cousin.

In my seat was a small forgotten bunch of pink roses.

RED IN THE MORNING

A child tosses in his sleep.

The highly polished furniture reflects the highly polished face. Toys are stacked in the corner of the room, where they have been tenderly put to bed many hours before. The canary sleeps behind a cover so recently handled by sticky fingers. Mother and father sleep on, in the comfortable thought that everything is secure.

Downstairs, the breakfast things are set out ready for the next morning. No, this morning; it is three o'clock already.

A dog howls, a cock crows, and the sun, prompted by the noise, begins its ascension of blood.

A wind blows up, making leaves rustle as if the next moment may be their last. The deep, distant drone of thunder echoes through the early morning light. Another rumble rolls over the houses. And another. And another.

But no one awakes. No one moves. The people of Pompeii sleep on.

LIKE A YO-YO

"Here he comes! Get down!"

Miss Hemingway obligingly prostrated herself on the train floor as the little Swiss guard ambled past.

"Has he gone?" Miss Ashford whispered, peering cautiously about. They dusted their tweed suits, and sat up, looking as innocent as possible under the circumstances.

Miss Hemingway smoothed her grey hair into its severe bun, clamped down her uncomprising hat until it almost met the tip of her nose, and said: "I presume, Miss Ashford, that – considering this is all your fault – you can explain to the guard why we have no tickets?" She then swivelled the whole of her vast bulk around to confront Miss Ashford.

Miss Ashford decided that discretion was definitely the better part of valour, and retired strategically to a far corner of the seat to study the view of the mountainside and the nearby cows.

The two ladies had been friends since they were in their early twenties. It was not until their mid-fifties that they had daringly ventured on a continental holiday. And it was on this first day that they had taken a train up the mountainside.

Then they had decided – or rather Miss Hemingway had decided – that they would enjoy the brisk stroll down. Not quite halfway they had become a trifle fatigued, and Miss Ashford had timidly suggested they caught the train down from the halfway station. Miss Hemingway had clapped her heartily on the back and clumped off.

As luck would have it, there was a train already in the station and they had unthinkingly boarded it, settling themselves comfortably for the journey down.

After a few minutes the train had lurched into motion . . . up the mountain.

Miss Hemingway and Miss Ashford had gazed around in uncomprehending stupefaction . . . which

is why two British ladies of good character and re-
fined natures, came to be trundling up and down a
Swiss mountain, watching the local cows.

It slowly dawned on Miss Ashford that they were
in a foreign country, where they could not speak a
word of the language, with no tickets and worst of all,
Miss Ashford was sure it was not even a British-made
train. Tears rolled slowly down Miss Ashford's
cheeks, causing her companion to give a snort of dis-
gust.

"Miss Ashford! Although we are fortunate enough
to be on holiday, I must beg you to refrain from in-
dulging in such a feminine weakness as weeping."

Miss Ashford hastily mopped up her tears, and
smiled damply at her companion.

"Recovered?"

"Yes, thank you, Miss Hemingway."

"Then we must plan our escape."

"I don't think," said Miss Ashford doubtfully, "I
should be very good at that."

"Never mind. Never mind. Leave it to me. Not for
nothing was I president of the Salford Docks' Nature
Study Society."

"No, Miss Hemingway."

However, at the bottom, Miss Hemingway ducked
once more between the seats. Taking this as a sign of
defeat, Miss Ashford followed suit. Therefore, the two
friends began their second wearisome ascent of the
mountain, during which, tired by their long repetitive
journey, they both dozed off.

They awoke with a lurch, and crouching again as the
train reached the summit they were alarmed by a
deep chuckle behind them.

A small fat man gazed blankly down at them. He

said: "You have found somezing, no?" Then seeing the puzzled expression on the ladies' faces, continued: "I am sorry. My England is not good. I think I mean: you have lost nozzing, yes?"

A little out of temper at being discovered in such an undignified position, Miss Hemingway replied, a little acidly, "No. We're just crawling round here for the fun of it."

But Miss Ashford, who still had her bottom drawer intact at home, said with a smile, "We have no tickets."

"Ah, you have *lost* the tickets?"

Both ladies muttered something carefully inaudible, and sat down to watch the cows for the third time while the little man proceeded to crawl round the floor in search of the elusive tickets.

At the bottom, the Swiss gentleman looked a trifle mystified, and then said with a laugh, "Ladies, I 'ave here two tickets of persons who could not make the ascension. You would accept them, pliz?"

"Oh, thank you so much," said Miss Hemingway, with heart-felt relief. "Come, Miss Ashford."

At the barrier, they marched proudly up to the inspector with their newly acquired tickets. They were just about to go on their way, when the inspector called them back in loud and rapid French.

They did their best to oblige him by making conversation with : "Oui, oui, monsieur. Oui." At their feeble attempts, a broad grin spread over his face.

"I can," he added slowly, "speak English if you wish."

They nodded urgently.

He continued: "You have just come out of a train

coming down. You have just given me tickets for going up. You will explain, please?"

A ROOM OF MY OWN

When my sisters were asleep, and mother and father out for the night, I used to go into the garret and sit on the old horse-hair sofa. Here I would stay for hours, looking at the damp green walls, despising them for their dirt, yet loving them for their precious sympathy and solitude.

In the room which I shared with my sisters, there was plenty of physical space but I couldn't sit and think without being accused of sulking. I was sixteen when I decided to get a room of my own.

I was sixteen and seven months when I decided what to do.

I was just seventeen when I did it.

Mrs. Harris was a typical member of the affluent society. She was plump, prettyish, rich, and above all, she lived in a big house all by herself.

I didn't want to take it away from her – only to share it. I went round to ask her on Wednesday morning, and she laughed. She laughed so hard that I thought she was actually going to split her sides and die laughing, and let me have her house. Then she stopped laughing and started shouting. She said I was stupid. She said I was an idiot. She said I was mad.

So I hit her and she screamed. So I hit her again and I liked it, so I hit her with the poker; but then she stopped screaming, so I stopped hitting her.

A man came in with a nurse. He said Mrs. Harris had been screaming for over an hour, but I didn't believe him.

The nurse said she would look after me, but *I* didn't need looking after. It was Mrs. Harris. I told the nurse I was sorry for the mess I'd made and that I only wanted a room of my own. She smiled, and said she'd see I got a room of my own.

I like that nurse. She got me a room of my own. But I'm not by myself. They keep looking at me through the grid in the door.

I don't think I like a room of my own after all.

Notes on Illustrative Material
General:

Looking back over all these stories, we can get a general idea of the writer's style. Often the best sections are where the writer is getting right into the skin of a person, writing in the first person. This was something she found she could do well, so she developed it.

On the other hand, dialogue she found difficult, so often it is almost non-existent, the thoughts of the character making up for the loss. The vocabulary is not large: but here again, a weakness has been submerged by deliberately trying to squeeze the last ounce of meaning out of simple words. It is clear, too, that the writer enjoys exploring people's minds and the way they think. From this, probably come the two excursions into characters whose minds are deranged.

Notice, too, that the various first persons, although all female, and usually about the writer's age, are all individuals: they have one thing in common: they are all thoughtful characters, concerned with their very personal view of life. This is where the writer drops her mask and we have a fascinating glimpse into an-

114

other person's mind – which is the art, not just the skill, of writing.

Polar Bears

The conflict is completely internal: it goes on in the mind of the child whose ideas about polar bears conflict with reality. Because we have all had cherished illusions shattered, it is a topic of immediate interest.

The background is lightly drawn, and the main description confined to the two sets of bears: they are the most important, so the rest can be ignored. The details of the birthday presents are very revealing, both of the age of the child, and its character – the child comes very much alive in the refusal to be parted from the slippers.

Direct speech is kept to a minimum for two reasons; firstly, the whole tone of the story is representative of the child's thoughts and speech. Secondly, when the one direct speech line comes, it is all the more effective – and leads to the deciding factor – the sight of real polar bears.

The ending is straight, but moves us into the adult world: now the grown child is looking back at the first stage in growing up.

The whole story has a ring of truth about it, mainly because of the acute observation of the way an imaginative child will play with toys. It is, however, completely fictional, and was written as homework to the set title *Polar Bears*.

Grandpa

Although the whole story is just a joke, it has the same qualities as any other, with the exception of credibility. We do not really believe it, and for once it does not matter. We agree to believe it, to see what the final joke will be. The conflict is between Wilfred and Grandpa – but Grandpa is dead, which makes it more unusual.

Mainly the fun comes from the wording: "certainly the only time he had been dead"; "the air was tense with crossed fingers and gritted teeth"; "a face you wouldn't mind seeing on a toad", and the sudden circular ending. The framework of the story came from a lesson on this.

The main part about the ending is how much is left out: we are told just enough to make sure we understand – but we are never told that Wilfred is dead. A good example of allowing the reader to guess.

Blue Ending

Here the writer has tried to get right inside the character that is being portrayed. Certainly it is one of the most complicated stories, but whether it is a success depends on whether you can accept the peculiar train of thought of the central character.

Is there really a good enough reason for committing suicide? At first sight there is not: but surely part of the reason for suicide is that a person must be thinking in a very muddled way, and that is just what is happening. The girl's brother and his wife have stopped her "living" – and so she refuses to "exist". It is on the play of these two words – which apparently mean the same thing – that the story depends. It is rooted in the overtones of these words.

Notice how the phrases are repeated – the word "blue", too, is echoed again and again. Both help to hypnotise us into understanding the mind of the girl.

The thoughts run over and over in her mind, and in ours, too.

In fact, it comes as something of a shock that the story is in the third person. But it has to be – the death of the first person would be very odd!

The background is seen through the eyes of the central character: there is no dialogue, because the whole story is the direct thought of the character.

"Rain-drenched streets" and "sapphire embrace" are good examples of "doublets" – the second being the more striking.

Lastly, look at the real use that is made of punctuation. It becomes more than just divisions into sentences and paragraphs. It makes the whole passage work at the right speed. Read it aloud, and see how the punctuation forces you to read it exactly as the writer intended.

Antique Roses

Although the opening seems slow, a more rapid one would have been unsuitable for this softer, more delicate story. The whole style is gentle and flowing: long sentences and paragraphs and soft-sounding words. But the humour of "wasting time by being good" and the "laughing cousin" at the end, contrast with the graver tone of the dream.

By the time we reach the "tall head-dresses" we have been in the dream for some time. The descriptive sections, linked by the train's movements, are intense and gaudy, but distant. Not until the train stops are the figures really alive – as the dream gets deeper. Although much of it is general, it is the details that stand out and bring the scene alive. The repetition of "quiet" and "dignified" points the contrast between widow and mother.

The ending, of course, is a twist, which suddenly makes the title clear – and makes us think about the whole story again. "Was it a dream?" we are asked.

Red in the Morning

This contains a rather odd kind of conflict: between the writer and the reader. The reader wonders what is the point of this apparently descriptive passage, is kept interested by the hints of disaster in such phrases as "ascension of blood"; and finally the whole is made clear in the last line. In fact, it appears to have a twist ending. This type of story cannot be long: either the reader guesses, or loses interest – but it is quite effective at this sort of length. You might discuss whether it actually *is* a story – nothing seems to happen in it; yet it contains other elements that seem to insist it is a short story. But where are the central characters?

The details of description are carefully chosen: they must not appear too unusual or the point is given away. The facts were taken from a history lesson some years before: the canary was actually found in the ruins of Pompeii. Note how sharp the ending has to be: a word or two more and it would be spoilt.

The title is a cliché, which has been given new life by the new meaning it acquires. Remember that the word rhyming with "morning" is "warning": even this is part of the overtone of the phrase.

Like a Yo-Yo

A third person story, which contains far more in the way of characterisation. Miss Ashford is the more timid: Miss Hemingway the leader. Nevertheless, both are slightly cartoon characters: the elderly spinsters abroad, calling each other by surnames, travelling in an un-British train. There is some gentle fun being made of them, and also of the oddly spoken foreign passenger. The slight change in Miss Ashford, when accosted by an eligible foreigner, is again hardly serious.

The background of the mountain railway was acquired from actual experience on a school trip abroad; yet the story in its original form was of schoolchildren, and easily as it reads, this is in fact about the fourth version of the same basic plot.

The opening is brisk; essential background details being filled in in the sixth paragraph. The next five paragraphs bring us back, in time, to the opening.

The ending is a simple twist, which rounds it off more neatly than the simple gift of tickets, which as a deciding factor would have been too flat: a fault which appeared in the original version.

The vocabulary, with its overtones, is rather intricate in places. Miss Ashford "timidly suggested" the train: Miss Hemingway "clapped her heartily on the back and clumped off" – the distinction in their characters is held even in description of their actions. The title is intended to intrigue, yet fits the story.

A Room of my Own

From the start, there is something odd about all this. The odd-child-out of the family, who so desperately wants a room of her own. We expect the conflict to be between her, and actually getting such a room, and so the whole of the first three paragraphs are spent in increasing the tension.

The picture of Mrs. Harris seems crude, until we realise that it is not a description, but a biased statement deliberately phrased in clichés. The dreadful ordinariness of the "I went to visit her on Wednesday morning" and the increasing collapse of any attempt at complicated sentences, convince us that the girl really is insane. The style is so simple, that the full horror of "I liked it" comes out. Over and over again comes the phrase "a room of my own" – until the story rests on a sort of twist ending: the asylum cell. This time we have really another conflict: between the writer and the reader – can we guess at the ending? We think we can, but we only see the madness, not the neat link back to the opening. So we have a twist ending, which is also circular.

This story was written to the set title in an hour, as part of an English examination. One of the dangers was that a story to this title might have been off the subject – so the title has to be repeated frequently – it becomes a phrase that is on someone's mind: the mind of a lunatic.

Looking Ahead

SOONER or later, you will want to try writing something much longer than the general length of six hundred words that we have dealt with in this book.

As your stories become longer, you can increase the number of characters, and the complexity of the plot: so the longer story seems a very attractive proposition.

Unfortunately, you will soon find that it is more than twice as hard to write a twelve hundred word story as a six hundred. Difficulties multiply with length, so be prepared for some disappointing results early on.

Never start anything that you cannot reasonably expect to finish. An unfinished project is mainly wasted time, so try not to think in terms of novels yet.

Even so, you can bear the idea in mind – so long as you realise that it needs about an hour's work a day, for a year! If this does not appal you, then by all means go ahead – but you may well get more pleasure from a couple of hundred short stories, with no more effort.

Recognise your limitations, and you will avoid the worst disappointments.

Some further suggestions for class work:

Writing is a highly personal affair, and you are unlikely to get much profit out of trying to write with someone else. (Although there are two of us working on this book, you can see we have kept ourselves to ourselves!)

Planning, however, can be done as a group – a general theme can be hammered out in discussion, each person then working it out in their own way.

Similarly the same story could be written as through the eyes of various characters.

Where the whole class can join in, is on the criticism side. When you do this, it ought to be understood that you are never polite unless you really mean it. To praise someone's work insincerely is insulting and unhelpful to them. The thing is to look for what you think is best in their writing.

There may be a school magazine to which you can contribute. If not, then it may be possible to start one for stories only. You will probably find that this can be made into a commercial proposition: stencils and paper plus use of the school duplicator can make a magazine fairly cheaply. There is often a ready market among parents. Also, you will soon know if your stories are not worth reading: you will run out of customers.

If there is a Writers' Circle in your district, a few of you might be able to get an invitation. Usually such groups are very willing to encourage you, once you have shown you are keen and competent at school.

If you have found a real interest in writing, then it is worth realising that competent writers, not necessarily brilliant ones, are very much in demand. Newspapers always need writers, both on their staff, and contributing material on a part-time basis. Magazines need articles and short stories. Radio and television use dramatic material at an enormous pace. Advertisers need copy-writers: scientific firms need technical authors and writers for publicity material.

At least, it is important for you to realise how many openings there are: the next generation of writers must come from somewhere – and roughly speaking, there will be room for one person from every secondary school, every year, in some job which depends to some extent on writing ability.

It may encourage you to know that the author of the stories in this book was offered a full-time job in writing while still at school, and that at sixteen she is the trainee editor for a group of magazines. Others from the same form – boys and girls – are finding there are more jobs open to them as a result of their writing skill.

Remember, too, that many authors are only part-timers. Housewives, especially, manage to find time for short-story writing for women's magazines and children's books.

There are always good opportunities for those who are really keen. In fact, judging by some periodicals, it seems that keenness may be more important than competence!

Reading List

Alice in Wonderland	Lewis Carroll (*various editions*)
The Black Cloud	Fred Hoyle (*Heinemann* 1957)
The Book of Joshua	Old Testament (*Authorised Version*)
A Bullet in the Ballet	Caryl Brahms and S. J. Simon (*Michael Joseph* 1951; *Four Square* 1964)
Dr. Syn	Russell Thorndike (*Hutchinson* 1961)
Diary of Anne Frank	Anne Frank (*Hutchinson* 1960, *Pan* 1960)
Don't Do It!	Jane Hope (*Muller* 1947)
The End of the Affair	Graham Green (*Heinemann* 1951; *Penguin* 1962)
Henry IV, Part I	William Shakespeare (*various editions*)
I Capture the Castle	Dodie Smith (*Heinemann* 1949)
In the Abyss	H. G. Wells (*this is included in* Short Stories of H. G. Wells, *various editions including Penguin* 1958)
Ivanhoe	Sir Walter Scott (*various editions*)
King Solomon's Mines	Rider Haggard (*various editions*)
Moonfleet	Meade Faulkner (*E. Arnold* 1961, *Penguin* 1962)

No Highway	Nevil Shute (*Heinemann* 1953; *Pan* 1963)
The Picture of Dorian Gray	Oscar Wilde (*various editions*)
Pride and Prejudice	Jane Austen (*various editions*)
Quatermass and the Pit	Nigel Kneale (*Penguin* 1960)
Rebecca	Daphne du Maurier (*Gollancz* 1939; *Penguin* 1962)
The Small Back Room	Nigel Balchin (*Penguin* 1958)
The Snow Goose	Paul Gallico (*Michael Joseph* 1941)
A Tale of Two Cities	Charles Dickens (*various editions*)
The Thirty-Nine Steps	John Buchan (*various editions*)
The War of the Worlds	H. G. Wells (*various editions including Penguin* 1941)

*Many of these titles are also available in paperback editions
that have not been listed above.*

Index